Simple Truths
in **Music**
and **Life**

Also by Don Brown

Situational Service®—Customer Care for the Practitioner

What Got You Here Won't Get You There—in Sales!

Bring Out the Best in Every Employee: How to Engage Your Whole Team by Making Every Leadership Moment Count

Simple
Truths
in **Music**
and **Life**

Don Brown

For further information, contact DonBrown.Org

2520 West Delhi Road
Ann Arbor, MI 48103 USA
(734) 669-4363
Kelly@DonBrown.Org

This is the story of a five-year musical journey with an icon, friend, and mentor—Uwe Kruger. I dedicate this work to you Uwe. You make many lives good.

"Don, don't worry how you come across or what the world thinks ... it's your path. As a musician, you should be the last to care."

— *Uwe Kruger*

Introduction and Acknowledgments

I treasure my friendship with Uwe Kruger. Uwe is a singer, songwriter and guitarist extraordinaire who has brought me to amazing—for me—musical heights. But it all started by accident.

Six years ago a good friend of mine, Davis Holloway, invited me to the inaugural three-day "Kruger Brothers Music Academy" taking place a few months out. Davis was a banjo player and thought I might like to join him for the weekend. He was such a good friend that I agreed right then and there. Davis was ill at the time though, and when that first Academy finally rolled around, he was physically unable to make the trip. I did make the trip and each evening I'd call Davis so that he might vicariously sample the power of the experience. A month later, Davis lost his battle with leukemia. I forever thank Davis for leading me to this path. "I appreciate ya."

I've attended every Kruger Academy since. And after the first two years, I approached Uwe with the idea of writing a book about my musical journey with him. He modestly replied that he wasn't too sure anyone would care about his take on music. I told him at the time that he might be wrong. Now I know he was.

The result you now hold in your hands, a collection of ninety-four "simple truths" in music and life—and it is designed to fit into your instrument case! These are brief observations that are uncomplicated and succinct, yet profound in their impact. While they were discovered along a musical path, they also carry important parallel lessons on everyday life. Enjoy!

Thank you Uwe for the beautiful journey—and it aint over!

— Don Brown, December 2016

I'd like to add heartfelt acknowledgement and appreciation to Jon Wilson for his invaluable contribution to this work. Thanks and love as well to Colleen, Natalie, Kelly, Katie, Doug and John.

The Kruger Brothers

Born and raised in Europe, Jens and Uwe Kruger started singing and playing instruments at a very young age. Growing up in a family where music was an important part of life, they were exposed to a wide diversity of musical influences. The brothers were performing regularly by the time they were eleven and twelve years old, and they began their professional career in 1979. Jens' and Uwe's first public performances were as a duo, busking on the streets of cities throughout eastern and Western Europe.

CBS Records contracted with Jens and Uwe when Jens was just seventeen years old. Several years later, the brothers teamed up with bass player Joel Landsberg, a native of New York City who also had a very extensive

musical upbringing in classical and jazz music (studying with jazz great Milt Hinton), thus forming a trio that has been playing professionally together since 1995.

"The brothers," as they are called, moved to the United States in 2002 and are based in Wilkesboro, NC. Since their formal introduction to American audiences in 1997, The Kruger Brothers' remarkable discipline, creativity and their ability to infuse classical music into folk music has resulted in a unique sound that has made them a fixture within the world of acoustic music. The honesty of their writing has since become a hallmark of the trio's work.

Uwe Kruger

Uwe Kruger, lead vocalist and guitarist for the Kruger Brothers, has been playing music since early childhood. When they were very young, Uwe and younger brother Jens would place a guitar on the floor between them and play it together, one brother taking the upper three strings and the other the lower three. Uwe was introduced to American folk music through the brothers' father, who would bring folk music records when he returned to Switzerland from business trips to the United States.

For more than forty years, Uwe has been playing guitar and singing as a professional musician. Over the course of his career, Uwe has developed range and versatility—instrumentally and stylistically. Today, Uwe astonishes audiences with his blend of guitar-picking styles. His rich, resonant, and mellow baritone voice has an uplifting effect on all who hear him sing. Uwe has been influenced by a diversity of musicians, ranging from Doc Watson, Jerry Garcia, and Eric Clapton, to Beethoven, Bach, and Brahms. Watching and listening to Uwe's unique style, a blend of flat-picking and finger picking, is a fascinating experience. Uwe loves playing "in the moment," and his guitar improvisation during live performances has listeners sitting at the edge of their seats in excitement and anticipation.

Don Brown

Don Brown dedicates his career to "helping people with people" in leadership, sales and customer service. Bilingual and experienced at the executive and line-level alike, you see the results of his work across dozens of industries, including brewing, automotive, airline, banking and medical equipment.

Speaking, writing, coaching and selling to the best—Ford Motor Company, Anheuser-Busch, United Airlines, Harley-Davidson, Jaguar Cars, Hilton Hotels and many more—Don takes great pride in long-standing customer relationships (some running well over twenty years).

Don cherishes his start with Paul Hersey and Marshall Goldsmith, and has authored

books with each; *What Got You Here Won't Get You There—in Sales!* with Marshall and *Situational Service®—Customer Care for the Practitioner* with Dr. Hersey. Don's most recent book, *Bring Out The Best in Every Employee: How to Engage Your Whole Team by Making Every Leadership Moment Count,* is now joined by *Simple Truths in Music and Life,* a work that has led him to include the guitar in special keynote offerings.

Contents

Second Movement—PRACTICE

Third Movement—CREATE

Fourth Movement—PERFORM

Coda—SING

Creating Order Out of Chaos

What do you SEE when you play that song?

Discover What You See

"Don, what do you see when you play that song? Don't memorize words, discover what you see and the song is yours!"

— Uwe

I went for an afternoon's guitar lesson with Uwe Kruger at his studio in Wilkesboro, North Carolina. It was just the two of us in the building. We'd warmed up for a short while and he smiled and said, *"Would you play something for me, Don?"* Foolishly, I hadn't come with anything in mind to work on with him. But just as Maynard Holbrook *"loves them sad ol' songs,"* I too am a fan of heartbreak and sorrow music—songs by Hank Williams, Ray Price, Patsy Cline. Those are the classics, but I thought for a minute and decided to play a more recent Tim O'Brien piece of that same genre that I'd been working on called "Late in the Day." The lyrics talk about pouring whiskey over ice, trying to go back to a better time, and being with someone who's no longer there. Sounds like a familiar story line, right? There are countless classic and contemporary songs about alcohol and drowning misery— but there was just something special about Tim's song that spoke to me, so I played it for Uwe.

Unfortunately, it came out just like a thousand other songs that involve drinking, leaving, and loss. To say the least, I was uninspiring in my rendition, and we both knew it.

Uwe was quiet for a minute. He was smiling and kind as always, but he said nothing at first. He then asked me, "Don, what do *you see* when you play that song?" I have to say I was ... speechless. I reluctantly admitted to him that I didn't know what he meant. Along with a couple of lame excuses for my flat performance, I admitted too that in playing someone else's music, the hard part for me was keeping track of the lyrics. Uwe's smile widened as he said, *"Don't memorize words, Don,* **discover what you see** *and the song is yours!"* That ended our discussion of the piece and we moved on, but I kept coming back to Uwe's unusual question: what do I *see* when I sing?

As an auditory by nature, someone who processes the world through his ears, I'd *never* consciously thought about what went past my mind's eye when I heard or played a particular song. Total disclosure? Through the years, I had made somewhat of a habit of ridiculing music videos. I felt that all things visual had little to do with any given song. After Uwe's question however, during my ten-hour drive back to Michigan, I began to consider what I *saw* when I thought about "Late in the Day." I came to realize that, for me, the song wasn't about drinking in a lonely honkey-tonk, or cheating, or leaving in any traditional sense.

I come from a Scots-Irish family of four siblings. My parents had just celebrated their sixty-fifth wedding anniversary. And then, my father passed. My folks were always the model of stability and moderation. It seemed that just about every single evening during those sixty-five years, mom and dad would have a whiskey together. Not two, not three. One. Theirs had been a long-running ritual of a single drink together to mark the end of each day. Now mom was alone though, and I realized that what I *"saw"* when I played the song was an 83-year-old woman desperately trying to recreate one of her life's cherished rituals. Alone. By herself. *That* is what *I* see now when I play "Late in the Day." That is what it means to me personally. Picture that now as you read the lyrics to its chorus:

"Now I pour whiskey over ice
Put my feet up and close my eyes
I try to listen to what my
heart might say
Try and find the rhyme
To take me back in time
And be with you here
Late in the day."
— © 1987 by Tim O'Brien

Now *that* is a whole 'nother piece of art. I have no trouble remembering the lyrics. There is no mystery as to what I *see* when I play the song, and as a result my performances of it tend to be anything but uninspiring. Listeners now approach with excitement, shining eyes and warm words of appreciation, all because of one simple question, *"Don, what do you see when you play that song?"* A very different world is created now—all from the power of one simple truth; "**discover what you see.**"

Let me add too, simple truths apply to every part of life, not just music. This first simple truth is about making a message your own, and not just mindlessly parroting the words of another. In music, life, leadership, or even parenting—how effectively can we connect with another person, if we do not infuse our message with any meaning of our own? How many of life's performances fail to inspire? Sadly enough, perhaps the majority.

Uwe has been my teacher, mentor and my friend for a number of years now, but the very next time we spoke after that lesson I asked him if I might document my journey with him. He, of course, said yes with an open heart. The result of this journey is what you are reading now, with dozens of quotes ... dozens of powerful simple truths. They are now yours to enjoy and apply. However, *simple* doesn't always come *easy*.

Create Order Out of Chaos

> **"Our brains hate chaos. Your job as a musician is to create order out of chaos."**
>
> — *Uwe*

The first time I heard Uwe speak of "order out of chaos," I knew the concept would hold personal relevance—I just didn't know how personal. Uwe's guidance echoed the words of Yehudi Menuhin, arguably one of the finest violinists of the twentieth century. Menuhin defined music, like language, as simply a lens through which we make sense of sound. I guess that by default, my purpose in writing this book is also my conscious effort to "***create order out of chaos.***" I am a writer by trade. I speak, write, and coach people for a living. This is my fifth book. Over the last ten years, I've finally been able to articulate— and to live—my life's purpose. In my work, I essentially try to give gifts to others that cannot be repaid. Simple as that. And with this book, my desire is to help you with your musical practice—and with your life. That is my gift to you. My goal is to help you to discover the powerful simple truths that my journey with Uwe Kruger has revealed to me —and to apply them to your music, to your relationships, and to your life. During my research and writing, I surveyed and reached out to hundreds of students and friends of Uwe, I reviewed several years of Uwe's lessons on video, and I even secured English subtitle scripting from a Swiss television documentary on Uwe and his brother Jens. I gathered all I could, all in search of "simple truths in music and life." I've revealed two of those truths in this Prelude, and I have ninety-two more for you! You can read this book from start to finish, or simply open it up and enjoy the quotes and simple truths out of sequence. Throughout the text, any simple truths are always displayed in ***bold italic*** and you can also refer back to the table of contents to see a listing of each of the simple truths along with its page number. The interviews, conversations, academy lectures and personal lessons have all been transcribed, reviewed, and then run through text analytics software to help me discover patterns of frequency and sentiment—all to ***create order out of chaos***. Just about everything we do in life involves coaxing order from chaos—building a career, raising a family—why should our musical practice be any different?

And how much I've learned along the way! There are stories of a young boy in the attic dormer in Switzerland, of a fourth grader who, with his brother, took instruments to school to perform "You Are My Sunshine" on a rock wall at recess, of a first band called the "Undertaker Skiffle Company," and of countless performances on the streets of Europe and on cruise ships at sea—and finally of inspiring performances all across North America.

"Simple Truths in Music and Life" is my attempt to document for you my journey with a singer, songwriter and guitarist extraordinaire that has brought me to amazing musical heights. Let me perhaps ***create order out of chaos*** on your musical journey—on your *life's* journey.

The structure of this entire work is to give you the benefit of my journey over the last five years; to offer you dozens of short, simple, truthful statements about music and life. Embrace it as a work by a musician for musicians—and non-musicians alike—with lots of great advice about life along the way. It is my pleasure to share it all with you. Enjoy the four movements that make up this composition. Consider them a personal, enthusiastic exhortation from Uwe himself:

Play, Practice, Create, and Perform!

First Movement

PLAY

It is Supposed to be Fun!

Music is a playful thing.

**Become
like a
child
again.
Be
happy,
just
play.**

If you join a poker game, you don't go there to win or lose money, you do it to play poker.

Chess at any level is still a game.

Playing a guitar should be like that.

It's what makes us human.

You don't always have to progress, you can play for the sake of play.

When you are playful, creativity happens, collaboration happens, inspiration happens.

You can get out of doing dishes by playing guitar!

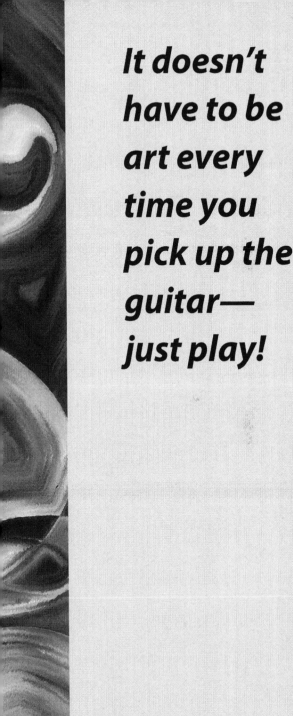

It doesn't have to be art every time you pick up the guitar— just play!

*When you
play music
you get into a
consciousness
that is caring.*

*You care for
your music.*

When you play, technique matters— not tricks.

Without a doubt, the idea that resonates most often within Uwe's musical vocabulary centers on the idea of "play"—not just the technique that it takes to create music on the instrument, although that's in here as well, but in every sense of the word. *Play* as an exercise or activity for amusement or recreation; *play* meaning something done in fun or jest as opposed to seriousness; *play* as an action or activity in the conduct of a game or pastime; or *play* meaning to employ oneself in diversion, amusement or recreation. Uwe's use of the word *play* frequently evokes the image of a child— of child's play or of being childlike, and of playing games as an expression of our humanity. To begin this first movement, let's explore some of the simple truths to be found in the word "play." I'm willing to bet that you once learned and lived many of these truths, but lost them somehow along the way to adulthood. I know I did.

Put the Play in Playing Music

> **"Let's put the play in playing music. It is supposed to be fun!"**
> — *Uwe*

Think of this moment; possibly the highlight of any musical lesson or workshop. Think about the time that comes for student to play for teacher, and maybe for a couple dozen classmates. What could be better? Everyone there has your best interests at heart. Your instructor and peers support you. They await your song with warmth and pleasant expectation, knowing too that they're going to be playing next. You've been excitedly anticipating the opportunity to show them all what you've been working on—until your name is called. Suddenly you forget to breathe. It starts to get really warm in the room. Your hands, arms, shoulders, and neck begin to cramp. Your heart rate doubles and, feeling a little sweaty, you forge ahead and take your turn in the hot seat (it's aptly named). You play. You sing. *It's a train wreck!*

Or, consider another moment. You're all alone this time. It's 9:00 p.m. It was a really long day at work. You're tired and you feel like nothing more than going to bed. Instead, being the disciplined trouper that you are, you get your instrument out of the case. You don't even bother to tune it, instead you jump right into fifteen minutes on autopilot, carelessly running through the half dozen songs you've been noodling with lately. It was barely enough time to warm up, let alone make any real progress. It didn't even feel good or sound good. In fact, you might even call it painful. You went through the motions, but you're more exhausted *after* playing than before. You regret not just going to bed. But at least you got some practice in, right? You put the instrument away roughly, maybe even a little angrily.

In each of these two scenarios, there was no "play" to be found. There was no fun being had! In the first case, you walk away bewildered as to why your performance didn't go as you'd imagined, and thinking, for crying out loud, why did I freak out the way I did? It happens to us all. You've played the song a dozen times—but never as poorly as you just did for your friends and mentor. It was highly disappointing, and it was depressing rather than uplifting.

In the second scenario, you wasted an opportunity to catch up on some sleep, to simply treat yourself to a little recovery after a long day. Instead, you made a chore out of making music. A drudgery of a hobby. Misery out of mastery. It's frustrating. Why didn't you just go to bed? And to add insult to injury, you probably couldn't even get to sleep afterwards just thinking about it.

Sometimes we take the play or fun *out* of making music, instead of putting the play or the fun back *in*. This foundational simple truth says so much: "***Put the play in playing music,*** *it is supposed to be fun.*" Music—and life too—is supposed to be fun. I know it's difficult to keep the fun and keep the faith when life becomes a burden, when earning a living, raising a family or maintaining our health take a hit from unforeseeable events. But have you ever noticed that some people seem to *choose* a good day regardless of what's going on in their life? And let's not forget too—we make a conscious choice to put music *into* our lives. Not everyone does it, and no one is forcing us to do it. This distinction is foundational to Uwe's approach. For his students, and clearly for himself, keeping the *play* in playing music comes up over and over again. Sitting in a hotel lobby with him one time Uwe told me, *"When we play guitar it's not about having to achieve something before we have fun ... we are given the fun the moment we pick up the instrument ... don't lose the fun, just be happy with it."* In the car driving to his show in Asheville, North Carolina on another evening he added, *"Did you know you can get out of doing dishes by playing guitar?"* Guess what? He's right! I in fact regularly *do* get out of the dishes by playing the guitar and singing a song or two after supper (do you?). When I showed the dishes quote to my wife, she laughed and said, *"Yeah, he's got you pegged all right!"*

Now, before we move on from this simple truth, I want you to think about it a little more. Take it a little further. **Put the play in playing music**. Uwe is simply saying be *happy*, have fun and just play, right? But, sometimes playing music isn't fun. Sometimes it makes us distinctly unhappy. Why does that happen, why doesn't it always make us happy? Perhaps a simple truth of my own can help here.

———————

You Bring Happy

> **"There are lots of jobs that can pay you and challenge you—but you bring happy."**
> — *Don*

In my most recent book I included a lot about the idea of happiness and where it comes from. A woman I was coaching at the time had arrived at a career and life nexus. Closing in on fifty years old, she had been considering changing jobs. She told me, *"I want a job that challenges me, compensates me well for my work, and one where I can be happy."* I responded, *"There are lots of jobs that can pay you and challenge you, but **you bring happy**—you make the choice to be happy, or not."*

This is a simple truth I learned through coaching and helping others. **You bring happy** *to* the job, not the other way around. In fact, the number one predictor of satisfaction at work is what is called "core self evaluation." It's not the boss, it's not the money. How happy you are in your work, regardless of what you do for a living, is dependent upon how happy you are with *yourself* to begin with. **You bring happy**—to work, to life, and to your music.

Uwe agrees; *"If someone believes that when they just learn to play the guitar a little better, that's when they will be happy—they are wrong. They will make the choice to be happy with or without the guitar."* This caution also echoes the wisdom of another mentor of mine, Marshall Goldsmith, who urges us to be happy *now*. Most of us suffer the great western malady of *"I'll be happy when"*—I'll be happy *when* I get the new job, *when* the kids are finally in school all day, or *when* they finally get out of school, or *when* I can retire. The list is endless. I've known individuals that genuinely believed they couldn't be happy until they retired. They finally did retire—and died within months or a few short years.

This same dynamic can also slip into our music if we let it. I'll be happy *when* I can comfortably make bar chords, *when* I can play up the neck, or *when* I can finally play "Black Mountain Rag!" In researching this book, a friend revealed to me that he had been putting off getting back to playing guitar like he did in his teens and 20's.

Work, family, life, and his health—they all conspired to keep music at bay for thirty-five years. He figured he'd get back to music *when* the kids grew up, *when* he retired. He would play again *when* he had the time. He paused then, and wistfully admitted to me, *"I could have been playing music every one of those thirty-five years, Don—and I will never get them back."*

Don't fall into a loop of *"I'll be happy when"*—of waiting for the guitar, the piano, the banjo to make you happy. *"When"* never comes—or it will come too late. **You bring happy.** It *is* a choice, and life is short. Take a quick moment here and run some simple math. Multiply your age by 365. Subtract that total from 30,000—the result is the approximate number of 'wake ups' you have left (*if* you are lucky)! **You bring happy.** Bring it now. Please.

So it is up to us then. *We* make it fun. We bring happy to music and to life, and we want to be happy *now,* wherever we happen to be on life's path. OK then, *how*? I have always been a *"so what—now what"* kind of guy. There's no question that the healthy approach is to put the *play* into playing music. But here is the $50,000 question: what do I *do* about it? *How* do I make it happen? How do I make sure I bring happiness to the instrument, to my work, to the time I have left with my family and friends? *How* do I put the "*play*" in playing music? How do I make sure it's fun, or as close as I can get?

There are three words that have emerged over my discussions with Uwe about *how* to do it, three words that when understood, accepted and adopted can give us our best shot at bringing "happy" to music and to life. The words that matter are *child, game,* and not surprisingly, *technique*. Let's talk about them right now. Let's take "child" first.

Feed That Child

> **"Don, how did you feel when you were very young, before you ever fell in love? Feed that child in you!"**
>
> — *Uwe*

Uwe's remarkably simple and undeniably powerful "how-to" here is to first **feed that child** within you. If you spend any time with Uwe, you too will hear repeated reference to children, childlike, child's play and the child's voice and spirit within all of us.

> **"Become like a child again ... it brings warmth and humanity, and lets go of arrogance ... it lets you put some of yourself into your music ... when you pick up a**

guitar you are ten years old again, and you won't ever grow old...we are born perfect, a child can fall down a staircase and not break anything—when we grow up and take ourselves too seriously we fall down and break everything!"

— *Uwe*

Sound familiar? Does it resonate with a story from your own childhood? Do you remember J.M. Barrie's "Peter Pan: The Boy Who Would Never Grow Up"? The Scottish playwright wrote the story of Peter Pan in 1904, but the creation applies today more than ever before. Add to it that there is now such a thing as the time-technology paradox that seems to deaden the child in all of us. The paradox is that along with all the convenience that mobile and wireless advancements provide us come endless distractions and a virtual anesthetic that may never wear off. Are we perhaps losing the child within? Uwe's admonition to wake up and feed that child now comes just in time.

When I think of the child within me, the first image I see, actually my first conscious memory, is that of the three year-old me, not a worry in the world, proudly marching alone down the center aisle of Hillcrest Church in Detroit, singing at the top of my lungs. It was a mother and child talent show in 1959, and to this day I clearly remember the lyrics.

When I think of the child in me, I also remember a friend's father allowing us to play on a brand new trampoline in the mid 1960's. He allowed it only *if* we would dig a hole in the backyard some 6' by 12' and 4' deep to set the trampoline down into. He figured that when we took the inevitable falls at least we'd start at ground level. What he hadn't considered was the fact that he had us dig the hole and set the trampoline only 20 or 30 inches away from the garage! I remember the unrestrained glee with which we jumped off the garage roof onto the trampoline. Have you ever double-bounced someone on a trampoline? Have you ever double-bounced someone on a trampoline when coming down from 10 or 12 feet in the air? It's a wonder the "child in me" even survived!

And how do I now feed that child? One way we can do it is by performing songs that recall these moments from our youth. Consider the song by Guy Clark called "The Cape." The lyrics of the first verse tell of an eight-year-old boy climbing up on top of a garage and jumping off! That's how I feed that child.

Every time I sing "The Cape" I think of jumping off my buddy's garage onto the trampoline. I *feed that child* within me by joyfully watching or mimicking my comedic heroes; the Three Stooges, Jerry Lewis, Jim Carrey, Mike Meyers, "Napoleon Dynamite" and lots of others—including any one of our countless Scottish relatives. I do this much to the groans of those who know me well and therefore have to listen to it often. I am OK with that. I also *feed that child* within by regularly turning off all of the annoying auditory notifications on my phone, by removing as many apps as I can and unfollowing people on social media networks who only post to provoke. My technology mantra? Unfollow, unclutter, and unsubscribe. I safeguard that child within me by limiting and carefully selecting the messages to which I expose that child.

What is the child within you like? What does he or she warmly recall from your early days? What was that first joyful memory that you still carry throughout your life? Recall it right now! That voice that responds within you is the voice to encourage, to feed, and to listen to. Uwe once told me:

> *"Don, before you're a teenager, you are the master of the world ... and as soon as you grow up, you realize you're not and the fears start to come on—'Am I good enough? Am I too old for this?' Forget about that.*

When you pick up a guitar, you are twelve again and you won't ever grow old!"

— *Uwe*

Find the ways to **feed that child** in *you*. It's your child. Take the time to do it right *now* before you read any further! This is *your* book. Use the journal pages at the back of the book. Go there now. Write down what the child's voice deep within you has to say to you right now. What will it take to revive that child, to keep it healthy? Only you possess the answer. I told you what does it for me: what you write down now can take you back to that playground. **Feed that child.** It's a great way to **put the play in playing music**.

———

Make a Game of It

"Music is playful, it's one of the things we do to enjoy life ... make a game of it!"

— *Uwe*

The next mantra to take you back to a musical playground is the word "game." **"Make a game of it,"** Uwe once told me, and what a journey of discovery those five words started me on.

"Don, when you pick up your guitar I want you play with it. If you get in a poker game, you don't go there to win or lose money, you do it to play poker. It's a game! I watched a guy on TV playing poker just for the joy of it, and he was winning!"

"But, money isn't the driver. Chess at any level is still a game of chess. Playing music should remain like that—the ability to play games is part of what makes us human."

"When you look at music in the context of a game, you have to expect to lose as well as win. That's OK. Even with the guitar, one day you win, and the next day you lose. There are some days when I don't win—when it overpowers me and even hurts me."

"Every day is a new day, a new beginning. Consider music a pastime. You're out there for the joy and beauty of it, and I want you to make a game of it!"

— *Uwe*

Wow, it seemed simple when Uwe first hit me with it. **Make a game of it.** Nothing terribly complex, right? Just make a game out of music. Use the idea of music as a game, as the mechanism to **put the play in playing music**. Well, I found it led me to more questions than answers at the beginning. What does he mean by making a game of it? Just what *is* a "game"? *How* do I make a game of playing music, and *why* should I? *Why* will making a game of music somehow put the play in playing it? After a lot of digging, I believe I've found us some answers.

Let's begin at the beginning. For me, when I'm not sure of something, in any endeavor, I default to creating what I call an operational definition. Paul Hersey taught me this long ago, to essentially articulate a definition that will serve as the foundation of my thinking. In this case I started by laying down a definition that we can use for the word "game."

Game: *an amusement or pastime; a diversion; a single occasion of activity; a competitive activity involving skill, chance or endurance, played according to a set of rules, usually for your own amusement or that of spectators; a contest with rules, the result being determined by skill, strength or chance.*

That's a pretty broad operational definition, forty-eight words to be exact, and it tells us in general terms how to think about "games." A game is a diversion—it aint life and death. A game takes place in a single relatively brief session; they don't go on for days (except, I understand, for the game of cricket). There can be a competitive dynamic to games, even if it's just a game of solitaire—we're trying to "win." And finally, a game is played with purpose, in a set fashion, and it's played for the amusement of self or others.

Reading this definition over and over got me to thinking. If I'm going to **make a game of it**, if I want to devise a "game" to play when I sit down with my instrument, I wondered how will I do it and what will I do it for? What began to dawn on me right then and there was the fact that all games seem to have *two* things in common: *rules* and *rewards*. Let's take that one at a time.

Rule: *a guideline governing conduct or action.*

Think about it, there's always a set of rules in any card game, dice game, or ball game. Rules rule, from billiards to baseball to bocce. Sometimes there are lines painted on a table or the ground to guide our play. Some games even provide live direction in the form of umpires or referees, or callers as is the case with square dancing and contra dancing. I guess rules are what create **order out of chaos** for a game. Imagine tennis with no lines and no net—it simply wouldn't be tennis. The cool thing is, *we* get to write the rules that will govern this game.

Allow me to tell you the rules that I play by when I sit down with my guitar these days (that's the other thing; I get to *change* the rules whenever I want!). I have found that a checklist of five rules, plus or minus two, is a manageable number. It's enough to give me some structure, but it doesn't become unmanageable. Here are my current rules:

- **A Five-Minute Minimum.** I set a minimum rule for playing time of five minutes each day. Of course, I never play for only five minutes, but this minimum "requirement" gets me to actually sit down with the instrument.

- **The G Position Warm Up.** That's where I start. Uwe says he always starts with the 'G' position. I figure if it works for him, it's good enough for me—and it feels right too. It always has. I don't question it. I do know that any endeavor takes warm up; music, athletics, dance or yoga, you name it. Warm beats cold every time.

- **The Blindfold Re-Play.** I literally put on a sleep mask and try to recapture the last song I played. Uwe always said that we only need our senses of sound and touch to play a guitar. I believe him. It is the best possible exercise I can do to bring myself into the moment, to be fully present with my instrument. *Try it!*

- **One You Know.** Sometimes I stay blindfolded for this, other times it's too difficult. Just pick a song you know by heart, but *not* one that you know on the guitar yet. It can be from when you were growing up or one you've heard lately that just stuck in your head. Just play the melody, on several strings or just one as Uwe has had us do, and sometimes you can even play the melody on one string and use the string next to it as a note in harmony.

These are just four quick rules that I currently use to govern my time on task with my instrument. This is how I play the game lately, and I love it. I haven't even touched upon repertoire review and revision, or scales, electronics, song writing, lessoning, or any other number of items that might generate the rules that can help you *make a game of it*.

If You Measure It, You Will Change It!

Can I give you a "bonus" rule for improvement at any game? It's a simple truth I have isolated in coaching people in the course of my work: *if you measure it, you will change it*. What do I mean? Keep score! I mean to journal, to simply write down, to keep a log of when you spend time with your instrument. I don't care if you write it on the wall with a pencil, just make sure you make a record of it in some way. As you reflect upon your habits over time, the "score" of your game will become apparent. You'll learn when you tend to play more often and even when your game is more enjoyable. Write down the day and time, every time, when you pick up your instrument (or sit down to it). When you're done, give yourself a score of between 1 to 10 based on much you enjoyed the time spent with the instrument, "1" meaning you were bored, frustrated or not even present, and "10" meaning that you loved it, it sounded great or you finally mastered a piece or a portion of one. You'll start to see patterns as to what time of day is best, how long the "game" should last, and even when you should skip playing all together. Keep score, even if only for a short period of time. *If you measure it, you will change it!*

Setting a few rules is the logical first step to making a "game" of it. Stop for a minute here and go back to your journal pages. Jot down some rules to define *your* game, write down five simple rules, plus or minus two, to live and *play* by. In fact, I'd love to hear from you. Email me at 'Don@DonBrown.Org' and tell me the rules that make the game of music fun for you. Perhaps someone else can profit from your creativity? Take some time to write down *how* you can **make a game of it.** Then, come back to learn about *rewards*, about *why* you might want to do it.

All games have exactly two things in common: rules and rewards. The *how* and the *why*.

Reward: *the return for performance of a desired behavior; a positive reinforcement.*

Let's start right there. A positive reinforcement, a *return* on behavior. That is *why* we play the games we do. Rules tell us *how* we play a game; the reward is what we get out of it—and why it might bring us back to play the game again, and again. Most of us are driven to play music to fulfill one of three basic need categories; emotional, social or achievement.

First, *emotional* needs: what does playing the game make us *feel*? Think about it; when we're playing or performing music, we might experience feelings of curiosity, wonder, awe, mystery, excitement, adventure, pride or enjoyment. We might also feel frustration, loss, disappointment or even pain, but one thing is for sure—when we play music we know we are going to feel *something*. And when we feel, we know we're alive!

Social needs can also be met when we play. Whether it's at a jam, an academy or a lesson, you are *with* other people. Humans are unique in that much of what we do is either directed at or in response to another human being. Some musicians might tend to be loners, with social needs perhaps left unmet. For others that play an instrument, what better "people fix" can there be than to perform a song for an audience. As Uwe has told me many times, *"there is nothing more personal than to sing a song to someone."*

The final need category that might be the reward, that might be the driver to play the musical game, is *achievement*. Meeting goals, hitting targets or overcoming obstacles and just plain personal growth can all serve as a powerful motivational catalyst to pick up an instrument. It might just be the one that floats *your* boat. Whether sitting first chair in an orchestra, having a song that you wrote performed, published or recorded, or just hitting a less lofty target like finally mastering a song you've always liked—goal attainment is as good a reason as any. So, what drives *you?* What need will music satisfy in your life? What will bring you back to play again and again? Emotions, interaction, or achievement? Think about it for a minute—but this in only one man's opinion (mine), and I'd like to give you a better and more formal understanding of personal motivation.

The gold standard for what drives everything we do from within is called "intrinsic motivation theory," and the man behind it is Steven Reiss. According to his theory, there are actually sixteen things that can make us happy in life. After a study involving more than six thousand people into what made them happy, Mr. Reiss identified the following basic desires bubbling within all of us:

1. **Acceptance:** the need to be appreciated or part of a group

2. **Curiosity:** the need to gain knowledge

3. **Eating:** the simple need for food

4. **Family:** the need to take care of our offspring

5. **Honor:** the need to be faithful to the customs and values of one's family/clan

6. **Idealism:** the need for social justice and equity

7. **Independence:** the need to be distinct and self-reliant

8. **Order:** the need for prepared, established and conventional environments

9. **Physical Activity:** the need to work the body

10. **Power:** the need for influence and the exercise of will

11. **Romance:** the need for companionship, mating or sex

12. **Saving:** the need to accumulate

13. **Social Contact:** the need for relationships with others

14. **Social Status:** the need for social significance and standing

15. **Tranquility:** the need for emotional calm, to be secure and protected

16. **Vengeance:** the need to strike back against another, to get even

We've gone from three need categories—to sixteen desires! My aim is to simply shed some light. Take some time now to consider the need triad of emotion, interaction and achievement. Pick up a pencil and circle *one* out of emotion, interaction or achievement that you believe makes the game of music *FUN* and rewarding for you. Just one. Then, go back over these sixteen basic "desires" and circle *two* that you believe are the strongest desires for you when it comes to playing music. For me, as I write these words, I'd have to say that my needs for "achievement", "status" and "independence" are the strongest drivers for me right now. Those are my rewards; that's why I engage in the game of music. Now what about *you?*

Circle one word, circle two more words, and now go to the journaling pages at the back of the book and write 'Reward' followed by the three words you've circled. This is your game. These are your rewards. Write them down. Acknowledge them. Embrace them. They are what make you, uniquely *you*. Then put the book down. You've set the rules. You know your rewards—now go **make a game of it!** Have some fun. I'll see you back here in a little while to think about the final word that came up with Uwe in relation to "playing" music. That word is *technique*.

No Tricks—Technique!

"When you noodle, you don't really care what's happening. But when you play music, you get into a consciousness that is caring. When you care for your music, no tricks— technique!"

— *Uwe*

Now we're talking. It's all about our manner or *style* of play—playing via technique, not tricks. Let's gets some definitions working.

Trick: *an intent to deceive or cheat*

Technique: *the employment of technical skill*

How many times in life do we hear the phrase, "fake it til you make it?" I understand the utility of the phrase. The problem is, "fake it til you make it" can only have a positive impact in combating two specific circumstances; overcoming irrational insecurities, or reprogramming negative self-fulfilling prophesies. The phrase "fake it til you make it" can help with self-esteem, but Uwe's core message here is not about self-talk, it's about skills acquisition and is very clear:

> **"I see no use in teaching you to get away with something ... I want you to learn it right."**
>
> — *Uwe*

There is no lack of clarity in what Uwe asks. *No tricks—technique.* Uwe asks that whoever we happen to be, just play like that person plays; not setting out to deceive or "get away with it;" not trying to show how much you know, but simply playing from the heart—*your* heart. There is another Uwe-ism that I've heard many times, and I think you'll love it;

> **"We aint young, and we aint pretty, but we're as real as real can be!"**
>
> — *Uwe*

That is the foundational premise of his words, and yes, there is work involved in developing technical skill with your instrument. Work is a given in life, in any practice; forget about faking competence. In my work developing leaders, the "fake it" mentality is rampant. The problem is, if we're always faking it, if we're always trying to deceive others into thinking we know what we're doing when we do not, we will never *ask* for help, for guidance. The world is so complex, so ambiguous, that nobody can have all the answers. The leader of the future, the teacher or the parent of the future will all have to learn how to ask. They will learn not to fake it, but instead to work on developing competence with the help of others. The unexpected bonus is that genuine, purposeful labor can also be a *joyful* journey!

When it comes to Uwe's guidance around technique, the skill of making music on your instrument, I've gathered a multitude of quotes and simple truths. I've decided to split Uwe's advice into two categories— *conceptual* and *behavioral*—a few tips on what he might want us to *know* about playing and technique, and then specifically what to *do*. I'm giving it to you all at once, but as I've done throughout, I'll present Uwe's words, and then show how I interpret them. My goal is to put Uwe's words within the context of his intent as I understand it when I hear the words. Sometimes what we say isn't always what they hear.

Get yourself ready for an exhilarating ride. Get out your hi-liter. Get ready to learn *how* to play!

———

Conceptual: What To Know

Do Less, Not More

"You're doing way too much with the instrument. You're actually stopping the guitar from producing sound. Every time you touch the strings you make it stop sounding and it has to start anew. Do less, not more. Let the guitar do the work!"

— Uwe

Do you ever get frustrated in a jam session? There are lots of people there, and lots of noise. It feels like you can't even hear your own instrument, let alone be heard by any one else. What do we do? Play harder, play louder, and play more! How about when you're playing solo? You have a vision in mind of the piece you're playing, of what it should sound like—except that your vision of the piece is one being performed by four musicians on four instruments accompanying three voices. What do we tend to do? If you're anything like me you still try to play harder, play louder, play more. How's that working?

Do less, not more. Sounds pretty "Zen" doesn't it? But guess what? It works. First of all, in a group setting, doing less simplifies and removes notes rather than adding to the noise. It allows us to listen for space, for quiet in which to play, even if only for a note or two. And when we're playing solo, the instrument is permitted to carry fewer but richer tones, and we can better hear and project our own intentions for the piece. Think about it for a minute. As a parent, if I am constantly yelling, always louder in competition with a child, what message will come across? The child hears a meaningless, indistinct garble. Is that what I want for my family, for my music? **Do less, not more**.

Without a Mistake is Almost Impossible

> **"To play something fast can be easy. To play something slowly can be really hard. To play without a mistake is almost impossible."**
>
> —Uwe

I chose this truth as the final "conceptual" note around technique. In a minute, I'll get to Uwe's foundation of what he wants us to *do* regarding technique, but right now let's spend a minute with this quote to close out what Uwe would like us to keep in mind.

"*Without a mistake is almost impossible.*"
Perfection is a tall order! Playing a perfect piece; being the perfect parent; perfect brother; sister; friend; partner or associate is in fact *usually* out of reach for most of us.

Now, is that all that this is about, simply knowing that we're going to make mistakes? Perhaps, but I believe there's a deeper message here. I believe it has to do with self-forgiveness. Most of the people I come in contact with are far gentler with others than they are with themselves.

Forgive: *to grant pardon, to cease to blame or feel resentment, to excuse, absolve, release.*

We're all guilty to some degree. I think Uwe's message here is to simply be kind to *you*. *Play* music, and realize in the end, it is still a game. To play **without a mistake is almost impossible.** Don't worry about perfection, just let it bring you joy. Forgive yourself. Grant yourself a personal pardon. Take technique seriously—it matters—but then let it go and *play*!

> **"Never think badly about your own playing, otherwise why are you here? You're just like me or anyone else in the room. There is no need to put yourself down. Ever."**
> — *Uwe*

Behavioral: What To Do

You might think that this segment would be the easiest thing of all to write. Just record and repeat everything Uwe says about what he wants us to do when we play. Nothing to it, right? Except, are you familiar with his nickname? *"The Guitar Doctor."* It is his moniker and his approach to teaching. And, while a doctor's process of diagnose and prescribe works wonders, my job here is to try and create order from chaos and write it up. So when in doubt, I default to the "rule of 3." After combing through all I have on Uwe's approach to technique, let me propose the following structure for the basics on how he views the behavioral side of play. This of course applies specifically to playing the guitar, although many of these concepts apply to other instruments as well.

1. The Fret Hand; anchoring and potential

2. The Play Hand; the pick and the pendulum

3. The Total Body; comfort and energy

The Fret Hand—anchoring and potential. Let's get it started. To extend the "Guitar Doctor" analogy, Uwe's musical check up generally seems to begin with the fretting hand.

Anchor to Minimize Movement

"To play faster, you have to minimize movement, but it's not just about playing fast. I want you to hit all of the notes too—smooth is fast. Put your little finger down on the first string...keep it there and you have an anchor to minimize movement."

— *Uwe*

Let's grab another operational definition:

Anchor: *to prevent or restrict motion, a source of stability or security, to bind one structure to another.*

Take this operational definition—and apply it to the use of one or two of the fingers on your fret hand. *"Prevent or restrict motion ... a source of stability or security."* This is what Uwe is talking about. In a "C" chord position he advocates keeping your pinky finger planted on the third fret of the first string. You keep it there, and with your other three fingers you're playing the "C" chord position, the "F" chord or the "G". The pinky finger stays there, and in doing so, your fingers never stray far off the fret board. The less your fingers have to move, the quicker and more precisely you're able to play. Smooth is fast. The same applies to playing in a "G" position. In this case, two fingers remain anchored. The pinky finger is anchored to the same third fret of the first string, and your ring finger is anchored to the third fret of the second string. Your middle and index fingers and even your thumb then move to form the "G" chord position, the "C", and even an "A" and "D" chord.

Anchor to minimize movement. Minimal movement makes for smooth, and smooth is fast. The Krugers' label and company is "Double Time Music" for a reason. If you know them, you know they can play very fast, they play smooth and they hit all the notes. You can too, and there's another advantage to these anchoring techniques that we haven't even talked about yet.

Think about it. Perhaps you remember our earlier conversation about the fact that the instrument has to stop sounding every time we hit or lift off the strings. This break, no matter how brief, has to be bridged by your audience. Do it *for* them! Go back to another part of our definition of anchor, *"to bind one structure to another."* These anchoring techniques allow you to minimize movement, and they also serve as that seamless bridge between the 1, 4 and 5 chords. It becomes a drone to effortlessly bind one musical passage to the next. Effortless is smooth, smooth is fast. Smooth is sonically pleasing too.

Let's take these truths off the instrument for a minute. There are thought leaders that speak about keeping the important things in life front and center; Stephen Covey's *"put first things first,"* or Sean Stephenson's *"when life works."* I think **"anchor to minimize movement"** actually gives us a two-for-one in terms of leading an effective life. First, minimizing unnecessary movement is key to any kind of productivity, at work or at home, because it's about being productive and not just busy. And then, what are your *life's* anchors, the ones that bind one *life* passage to the next for you? Is it your spouse or family? Fitness habits? Your work? Comfort rituals? We all have our anchors. I know that music itself is one of life's strongest anchors for many of us. Being aware of our anchors helps to keep them strong, functional and smooth. Pay attention to them. Know what they are. Write them down. Speak of them to others; pray over them; whatever it takes for you to make them a larger part of your life. And then, if you want to strengthen the lives of others, *you build a bridge.* I have a friend who always says, *"If you want a better world, you go first. Help more, judge less."* Put another way, *you build a bridge.*

The fret hand—anchoring and *potential.* While anchoring itself increases capacity, there is *more!* Let's talk about how we can further build our playing potential through smarter use of that fretting hand.

Give Away 25 Percent?

> *"I've seen so many people play without their little finger. Why would you give away 25 percent of your fingering capabilities? Would a basketball player give up one quarter of their height?"*
>
> — *Uwe*

Twenty-five percent of our fingering capability given away. I admit it; I steered away from using my little finger at every turn for a long time. Total disclosure; I still don't use it one hundred percent of the time. The beautiful thing is though, anchoring is usually done with the pinky finger. It's just leaving it in place, non-threatening, but the whole time it's in place it's getting stronger. Uwe himself swears that the pinky is the strongest finger we have.

Start using it right now. At first, if you're anything like me you won't like it. But then you will come to realize how much mobility it gives you, and then you'll notice that the span from index to pinky is really very comfortable for two-fret patterns, especially across strings (much more so than index to ring). Do *not **give away twenty-five percent*** of your fingering capacity. You wouldn't knowingly give away a quarter of your life, your energy, your smarts, your speed. Don't do it to your music; start it up now! Let's close out fret hand technique with one final tip.

Play AT the Neck

"Keep your wrist straight. The guitar neck should rest on the base of the index finger. You actually play AT the neck ... like a piano keyboard."

— *Uwe*

Be conscious of it. *Rest* the neck at the base of your index finger with a straight wrist and you'll find it minimizes movement and encourages the use of the pinky finger. The mass of your fretting hand, the palm, is what will move less as you play. It takes less energy, and causes less strain, and ultimately less pain. Don't believe me? Try this test from another former teacher. Make a comfortable fist with your fret hand and hold it at your side as if you were carrying a suitcase with it. No strain, no pain, right? Now tighten the fist a bit, still hanging at your side. Now begin to draw circles with the fist. Keep the arm at you side like carrying a guitar case, but start bending the fist forward, back, left and right. You feel the strain on the muscles and ligaments on the top of your wrist and hand? Imagine that same strain repeated over and over. That's where fatigue and chronic pain begin. **Play at the neck.** *Try it!*

1. Fret Hand; anchoring and potential

2. Play Hand; the pick and the pendulum

3. Total Body; comfort and energy

The Play Hand; the pick and the pendulum. You've probably heard different nicknames or references for the left and right hands in playing a stringed instrument. Some refer to the left, or fret hand, being for technique and the right, or play hand, for expression. I've also heard it explained as the left hand being the mechanic, and the right hand the artist. There are differences to be sure, but Uwe simply tries to give us what to do and/ or how to do it with each hand to play more *efficiently*. And, with the right or "play" hand? His guidance centers around two concepts; the use and integration of your *pick* and then the idea of a *pendulum* that governs timing and contact with the strings.

The Pick and the Pendulum

"For your playing hand, it comes down to taking advantage of the pick and the pendulum."

— *Uwe*

Let's start with the pick first. Uwe explained that *"as you hold your pick, two parallel points should be formed by the pick and the point of your index finger behind it."* This took me a while to understand at first. What he's getting at is that your play-hand thumb rides parallel to the strings. If you look at where your thumb points when you play, it would be straight up the strings to the nut. Your play-hand index finger in contrast is pointing down into the sound hole. This then gives us both control and touch. There are two parallel points: the point of the pick, and the point of your index finger. Uwe's always trying to simplify with concrete examples of his conceptual guidance. With flat picks, his advice is also all about simplicity and consistency. Find a that pick you like, and then stick with it. *Buy 100 of them!*

Probably the most profound right-hand technique I've learned (but not yet mastered) from Uwe is that of finger picking w*hile* holding a flat pick at the same time. This *integrates* the two styles. By this I mean instead of finger picking with thumb, index and middle finger, he's taught me to use the flat pick as I normally would—and then adding the middle and ring fingers to pluck or brush the strings. His intent is of course to simplify effort and expand options. What I produce by integrating the flat pick into my finger picking style is that three-finger tempo and style, with a stronger baseline and the ability to play a melodic run with the flat pick when it's needed (or when I just want to have fun!). I'm about seventy-five percent proficient with this. I am still more comfortable putting the flat pick down and just using thumb, index and middle as I'd originally learned. But the potential I'll gain when I *do* arrive at ninety to one hundred percent dexterity with the addition of the pick is far, far greater. It's worth the investment to me.

And now for the *pendulum!* Several of Uwe's quotes come into play here, let me give you three at once to set the meaning of the "pendulum" in play-hand technique:

> *"Clocks were built very early on to be efficient. They found that the longer and more stable the pendulum, the more accurate the clock. In using your whole forearm, you have a longer pendulum and more solid timing in your playing."*

"Keep the fingers of your strumming hand open. If you constantly open and close them, you shift the weight of the pendulum that is your arm."

"You also limit the freedom of your right hand by always planting your finger on the pick guard. You stop the clock! It doesn't mean you can never do it, just be aware of it when you do."

— *Uwe*

You get the message? We're playing from the elbow on down. Now, I know there are accomplished musicians that appear to play only from the wrist down—the exceptions that prove the rule I guess. Or maybe it's just Uwe's opinion. What I think he is after with the pendulum analogy is consistency; removing variables and obstacles. The same way we strain our left wrist when we don't keep it straight, we do the same with our right wrist by putting all of the movement through it. Some of us have lots of bad habits to unlearn. This is one of them for me. A helpful mantra? ***The pick ... and the pendulum***.

1. Fret Hand; anchoring and potential
2. Play Hand; the pick and the pendulum
3. Total Body; comfort and energy

Total Body; comfort and energy. Some would believe that a stringed instrument requires a right and left hand, and nothing more. There *is* more involved, lots more. Let's put the capstone on technique; the *total* body experience according to Uwe. It's all about *comfort* and *energy*.

Play Where You Are Comfortable

"Play where you are comfortable. Where you are comfortable, the guitar will be comfortable; that's the rule."
— *Uwe*

Comfort: *to soothe or bring cheer; a state of ease and satisfaction; freedom from pain and anxiety.*

Just as much of Uwe's guidance around left-hand right-hand technique is targeted to avoiding or relieving strain, so too is his perspective on the rest of the "total body" experience. Literally, to **play where you are comfortable.** The right seat; the right room; the right time of day. There are a lot of physical success factors around comfort. Heck, I never eat within two hours or so before playing a game of soccer or any significant workout. I now do the same for my music. But comfort is both physical and psychological. "Free from pain or anxiety." Anxiety goes hand in hand with music. When we play, we disclose a lot about ourselves. We expose who we are. It's part of the beauty of it. And, at one time I would have had a couple of beers before playing for others, to reduce the anxiety. Sound like anyone you know? It doesn't work. When you self-medicate the "nerves" with alcohol, you also give away a portion of your skills ... the quality of your technique, even your presence with the instrument. Alcohol is a depressant. Granted, it can depress anxiety—it produces the opposite of anxiety—but it's a counter-productive state. What brings comfort then? Rituals. Rituals will help find your sweet spot; to **play where you are comfortable**. Uwe too has comfort rituals.

"I too have rules, or even better, rituals when I play. I start with a good set of strings. I get dressed right (my guitar sounds terrible if I wear fuzzy clothes). I clean my guitar, and I wash my hands. Actually, I hardly ever play without showering and getting everything ready. It's like any other person getting ready for work."

— Uwe

While most of us earn our living in some way other than playing music, I've found that preparing in a more *disciplined* fashion —approaching it as I would my profession —provides the comfort. It frees me of pain and anxiety; my rituals soothe and cheer me. What are the comfort rituals that you associate with playing? How do you prepare to play? Take some time now to think. Go to the journal pages. Reflect through writing. What are the patterns or innocent actions that seem to bring you comfort when you play music?

Happier in Motion

> *"The body is much happier in motion than at rest, and your music is just a translation of that rhythm of your heartbeat."*
>
> — *Uwe*

Total-body technique means both comfort and *energy!* So how do we get it? Where does it come from? It comes from movement— from "motion." **Happier in motion** *than at rest.* To my thinking, the first lesson here is all about energy and inertia ... the idea that a body at rest stays at rest, and a body in motion stays in motion. It costs energy to alter either state, and our bodies are built to move. Watch professional musicians when they perform—they're always moving. The more we move, the more we *play*. The more we move, the more energy we generate within.

This makes me think of my father. From his sixties on, he did less and less, and it's a common response to aging for many of us. The longer we're here, the more life "hurts" when we move. One strategy is to move less, right? If you move less, it doesn't hurt. The problem is, with this strategy then the less you move—the more it depletes you when you *do* move. What we focus on expands. If it's our limitations, they will grow. If we focus on what we *can* do, our capability grows. It takes energy to overcome inertia. Don't stop. *Keep* moving. Don't waste energy just trying to "get going" every time. *Keep* going. It doesn't have to be fast and furious. Uwe has a habit of saying;

> **"Play slowly. It's a form of meditation…every note is heard and felt. It is captivating, it's energizing. It fills you."**
> — *Uwe*

It fills you with *energy*. Movement energizes you and your music, and repeated contact with your instrument can energize you too.

> **"When your body is in contact with your instrument, there is a deep physiological connection. Your body experiences the vibrations of the music—at 100 hertz or only 5 hertz per second."**
> — *Uwe*

And finally, the ultimate energizer—*oxygen!* Breathing energizes and focuses too. When I work with groups on how to better interact and be present with the people they care about, deep and purposeful breath is the number one recommendation. It will turbo-charge your playing as well.

Don't Forget to Breathe

> **"Don't forget to breathe when you play. When you run out of breath, you have this split second when your concentration goes to your breath instead of your playing."**
> — *Uwe*

What a two for one; breathing feeds our focus *and* our blood cells! If you've ever practiced Yoga, you know that when the going gets tough, we forget to breathe. And, we just might pass out—literally or figuratively. **Don't forget to breathe** when you work or play.

Let's take a rest for a minute. A long rest. Let me close this first movement on *"play."*

What a ride it's been! Sixteen simple truths to this point, from **Discover What You See** and **Put the Play in Playing Music** to **Feed That Child** to **Make a Game of It** to **No Tricks, Technique** and **Don't Forget to Breathe***!* I mentioned that the word "play" comes up more often than any other in Uwe's lexicon. He and I talked a lot about play, and why and how it matters, and what it means to him. I hope you've enjoyed the journey so far.

One final truth that came up in our discussions of "play" is worthy of mention in closing. I'll let Uwe's words speak for themselves. It actually has to do with the *enemy* of play, and it matters a lot!

Fear is the Enemy

> **"Fear is the enemy of play ... to be tense, to be cramped up. This contraction—this panic—freezes movement. Panic is actually the fear of fear itself, and to lose it we need to play. We are born to play, but then programmed for fear. In order to regain looseness, recall how it was before becoming spoiled. Don't worry Don, just play."**
>
> *— Uwe*

PRACTICE

*What You Put
into Your Life*

Your practice is the ritualization of your life over time ... whether I'm a guitarist or a farmer, my practice is what I do in life.

In German, we make the distinction between "Üben" and "Ausüben." "Üben" is the "practicing" that alienates so many children to music. "Ausüben" is becoming a "practitioner" of something ... the practitioner versus the theorist.

A common definition of "practicing" is simply learning or perfecting a musical passage.

Practicing comes when you want to perfect a certain move ... to overcome something you are struggling with. For that you need to understand process.

Before you can play as well as Doc Watson, first you have to be as good a man as Doc Watson.

Just play what has stuck. Learn all of the songs you heard and loved when you were a teenager, when you first fell in love. Let that be your path!

I asked Uwe a very simple question: *"If you had to tell me just one thing about practicing, what would you say?"* That word, it turns out, came in second only to "play" in frequency within my research. It sure comes up a *lot*—and I believe it might be just as important in terms of Uwe's impact on my life's journey. You see, when it comes to *"practice,"* I now go with the *noun*, and I've virtually discarded the verb!

Your Practice

I took piano lessons for about six years when I was young. To this day, I can hear the echo of the following conversation (most days it seemed):

> *"Can I go down to the park (or, out to play, over to Tommy's house, to the movies)?"*
>
> *"Did you finish practicing?"*
>
> *"Oh Mom, come on . . . please??!!"*

The *verb* is really painful for most of us.

Practice: *to regularly, habitually, repeatedly perform so as to acquire or maintain proficiency.*

Sound like fun? It speaks not of our intention, of purpose, or enjoyment, but simply—work. For the majority, it just means thirty minutes a day—and in my case with the piano it was *most* days over a period of six years! That represented some *45,000* minutes seated on a wooden bench, dreading most every one of them. In fact, for adults too, this is the painful paradigm of "practice": habitual, repeated, performance to acquire proficiency. The phrase is just as uninspiring to an adult as it is to a child.

But fast-forward eight or ten years and you would have seen me taking flat-pick and finger picking lessons at Elderly Instruments while in college in East Lansing, Michigan. You would have seen me playing the guitar on the balcony, the front porch, in my room or even at my job as a security guard from 11:00p.m. to 7:00a.m. You would have seen me habitually, repeatedly—and yes, even *eagerly* seeking out that same proficiency. What changed? Without knowing it, I'd migrated from the verb to the noun. I didn't change "it", but unknowingly I'd changed how I think about "it".

A concept called "cognitive dissonance" is right-on relevant here. It's simply about the tension we feel when juggling two conflicting realities in our heads (such as, "I love music in my life—I want to get better, but I *hate* practicing"). My friend Marshall Goldsmith is a true thought leader in the field of positive behavioral change. Marshall long ago simplified this important concept for me with the following statement: *"Don,* with dissonance you either change what you're doing—or **change how you think** about what you are doing." In other words, you can change "it" or **change how you think** about it. As usual, it aint easy—but it sure is *simple!* I could give up music and stop practicing altogether. Or, I could change how I think about one or the other. Of course, Uwe's counsel here helps us with how to do just that!

———

What You Put In

> **"Don, your practice is what you put in your life! Your practice is the ritualization of your life over time … whether I am a guitarist or a farmer, my practice is what I do … how I conduct my life."**
>
> — *Uwe*

Uwe's first language of German also lends a hand in explaining the difference in perspective that we're getting at.

———

Choose Practitioner or Theorist

> *"In German, we make the
> distinction between 'Üben'
> and 'Ausüben.'
> 'Üben' is the 'practicing' that
> alienates so many children to music.
> 'Ausüben' is becoming a
> 'practitioner' of something—we
> choose practitioner or theorist."*
>
> — *Uwe*

So in first considering the word "practice" we have three simple truths in play; ***change how you think***, ***what you put in***, and ***choose practitioner or theorist***. Let's look at them one at a time.

The first—***change how you think***—again builds the case for operational definitions. How about, let's ***not*** use the definition of "practice" as a verb:

~~**Practice:** *to regularly, habitually, repeatedly perform so as to acquire or maintain proficiency.*~~

How about we redefine "practice" as a *noun*:

Practice: *a craft or profession, as in medicine or the fine arts ... routine action, a habit or behavior ... action or experiment in contrast to theory.*

How does *that* feel? All we do is change how we define and think about practice—and all the dissonance, all the discord just melts away. Your practice is now made up of your form, habit, method, process, system, tradition or custom. There is no dissonance there. Just change how you think about practice. Adopt the *noun*, banish the *verb*! Change how you think about "it."

Now for the second truth; your practice as **what you put in** your life. This is when Uwe's floodgates opened after I asked for "just one thing" about practicing.

> *"Don, your practice of music is like eating ... you do it to live!"*

> *"You begin your 'practice' in life the minute you realize you are responsible for your actions. But then practice is not a chore. It becomes how you live your life, your obsessions; it becomes like a prayer ... your reason for being."*

> *"Your practice is not limited to the instrument. It is a way of life ... the way of the saint, the wise man ... it's not work—it's a philosophy, a glad taking of responsibility."*

> *"Doctors have a 'practice' right?*
> *Lawyers 'practice' law. Those are*
> *ways of life; a practicing Buddhist,*
> *a practicing Christian, in your*
> *practice of those things, you are*
> *putting them into your life!"*
> — *Uwe*

What you put in your life. At some point between twelve and twenty-two, I quit practicing. Somewhere between Detroit in the late-60's and East Lansing in the mid-70's, between Mrs. Bryant's piano bench and a room at Elderly Instruments—I began my *life's* practice. I put music into it, just as I've put the Spanish language into it, the applied behavioral sciences and even the hobbies of soccer and trail riding on horseback. They're all what *I've* put into my life. This is my life's practice.

And now the third truth I've discovered about the concept of one's practice—that of *choose practitioner or theorist.* Uwe's words are very powerful here:

> *"Your practice is what you do. That*
> *is what being practical means,*
> *being practical versus theoretical.*
> *We choose practitioner or theorist. I*
> *could listen to and study the guitar*
> *all my life, but that doesn't make*
> *me a guitar player. By sitting in*

the garage, you are never going to become a car."

"As a practicing guitarist, I become a guitar player. I take it out of the case and I play it. That is how I become a guitar player. The other path is just accumulating knowledge without ever doing anything about it or with it."

— *Uwe*

Choose practitioner or theorist. Beginning to craft a life's practice means *doing* something. Yes, we study. We listen as well. But being a musician means *playing* a guitar, a banjo, a piano, violin, trumpet, saxophone or bag pipes! I know of a forty-year-old man who attended a wedding where he witnessed the father of the bride play and sing a song he'd written for his daughter. Having a young daughter himself, the man vowed then and there to one day write and perform a song at his own daughter's wedding. The very next Christmas, his wife gave him a guitar as a present. She even researched lessons and music stores for him. It has been almost four years since that wedding day. He has the guitar. He has lessoning books and CDs. He has yet to open the guitar case and take out the guitar. He has yet to begin a musician's practice.

I know another man who has attended dozens of Grateful Dead concerts. He's recorded and enjoyed them all over the world through several decades, as well as other bands that encourage their fans to record and exchange music. This man is a friend of mine, and a great guy. He *knows* the Dead. He can recite chapter and verse to any question you could put to him about the band, he even wrote and published a book entitled *Everything I Know About Business I Learned From the Grateful Dead* (check it out!). But, he's never played "Ripple" or "Uncle John's Band." He is a practicing university professor of business. He is a practicing writer, but he has yet to begin a musician's practice.

My friend will likely never play a single note of music on an instrument. And that's OK. Your practice being **what you put in** your life means you have *choices*. We can decide what to put in and what not to put in. I recall countless conversations with my three daughters about what they wanted to study in college, deciding what their major should be. I believe it's such a difficult time and process specifically because they are deciding what to put into their life, and conversely what they will *not* be putting into their life's practice. That's a tough call to make at twenty years of age. It's a tough call to make at any age, and the difficult part isn't what you *will* purposely include in your future—it's what you're ruling out with the decision. But, the good news? We *choose practitioner or theorist*, and no decision is final.

A practice will evolve. It will change over time, and *you* make the choices that guide the evolution. My own musical practice today bears little resemblance to what it was back at Michigan State. Think about it. Back then I was *"Don-Version 2.0"* ... today I am *"Don-Version 6.0".* How could I possibly remain the same! There is a Zen parable that theorizes that with every breath we take we pull in new oxygen cells. These new cells mix with our own chemistry so that *we* become new with each breath as well. The guiding mantra is *"new me"*—with every breath I take there is a "new me" born. The mantra is equally effective for accepting your present musical practice as it is, to just letting go of a bad golf shot on a previous hole and taking on the next shot with a clear head. What a great way to leave the past in the past—and embrace today for all that it is. As usual, Uwe's words are the perfect capstone:

> *"My own practice ... the job description so to speak is evolving. I'm deeply involved now with the synthesizer. I am creating music for a children's theater. Nothing stays the same."*

"I'm fascinated by electronica ... but for itself, not just to mimic 'real' sounds—our brains will make music out of the sound."

"I have a school in Zurich now, and soon I'll go about once a quarter to teach ... I need continued growth and evolution."

"Most people look at themselves as a static system. But if you stay dynamic, you stay young!"

"To gain something, you have to let something go. To add to your practice, you also have to subtract."

"At one time, my musical practice was playing in such a way as to sell the most beer for the house. I was ready to give up playing. Without evolution I was over it. I was done."

— *Uwe*

I think right now we can wrap up this portion of our discussion of a life's practice by taking it off the instrument for a minute. Simple truths in music *and* life remember, and the words that continue to echo for me here have to do with when Uwe called one's practice *"a glad taking of responsibility."* The paradox is that responsibility in life is often what silences the child within. It can take the play *out* of playing music. Yet our practice likewise only begins by gladly taking on responsibility. I believe it's in this *glad taking* of the responsibility that we safeguard the child within. Acting on purpose, with clear intent, we give ourselves the only viable shot we have at a vibrant, renewable life's practice —with a healthy, happy child intact within.

Consider Uwe's own practice and his glad embrace of responsibility within his life:

> *"My life and practice of life are different from most in that my practice is not dictated by children and family."*

> *"I have had to discover responsibility within myself to go through life. If you don't have children, you either become a saint or you become a drunk, and it is my choice to not become a drunk."*

> *"Neither am I a saint. I desire to become a voice for good, to follow a humane path. I am not selfish."*
>
> — *Uwe*

Uwe has thought about his life's practice. He is probably one of the kindest and most transparent individuals I know. His disclosure carries great power. Through his words, I too have been able to better understand my own dharma, my own life's practice and purpose. Think about your life's practice as you read further:

"Yes Don, your practice—if you are lucky—is your dharma, and once you lose any negative connotation to your practice then it becomes a joyful, playful, fulfilling way of life."

"There is nothing magical about the practice of music, it connects us ... but we are all connected by math and physics too."

"The more we see ourselves as caretakers of American music, as public servants, the more our practice matures."

"Maybe in the end, music is worth taking seriously, because it's one of the few things we have to cope with life. Some would say there's only music and religion."

— Uwe

Music *is* worth taking seriously. Your musical *"practice"* is worth taking seriously. Embrace the noun. Ignore the verb. Take responsibility for how you think about it. Take responsibility for what *you* put into your life. Let it be a *glad* taking of responsibility. And take a few minutes now on your journaling pages at the back of this book. Add *your* words, whatever comes to your mind about your own life's practice. Perhaps the significant elements that you put into your life that you can identify. Trust your gut and your inner voice. Write it all down.

Adopt Process, Not Practice

> **"Traditional definitions of practice only come up when you want to perfect a certain move ... to overcome something you are struggling with. For that, you need to adopt process, not practice."**
>
> — *Uwe*

Two very important new words emerge from this quote about "practicing" for Uwe, these words are *perfect* and *process*.

Perfect: *to bring to completion or perfection, to make flawless or faultless ... to improve, make better ... to bring to final form.*

This then is the never-ending goal with our music; to improve, make better or bring to final form. This could be our goal in reference to a song, to a passage or even to a single musical lick. Perfection is a tall order, but when understood incrementally, the *goal* of "perfecting" becomes apparent; musical accomplishment, excellence, and precision of play. Synonyms might be to complete, to finish or polish. But, what about "process"?

Process: a systematic series of actions directed to some end, action going forward, a series of changes that happen naturally.

If to perfect our music is the *goal*, then process is the *way*. **Adopt process, not practice.** Synonyms here might include the course, the means, mechanism, procedure or proceeding. The focus here is on this predictable series of changes that take place —a growth process—and it leads to perfect. **Adopt process, not practice.** We look to follow a process to our learning, perfecting, or mastering something, in place of simply "practicing." "Process" carries no negative or distasteful connotation as that which comes with "practicing." Change your definition, and then let's take a look at how Uwe sees this process of beginner to expert. I think you'll like it as much as I do. Let's take it one truth at a time!

Can't Help but Get Better

"Common definitions of practicing
are simply learning or perfecting
a musical passage. If you continue
to play honestly, and if you put in
the time, you can't help but get
better. There is no way around it,
perfection comes from repetition."

—Uwe

Just Not Enough Time Yet

"Don't think of your technique as
being good or bad, it's just about
not enough time yet. We're all on
the same playing path, I'm just
further along than some other
people on this path."

— Uwe

We Want Success Too Fast

"The biggest problem we have
when we learn guitar or anything
else is that we want success too
fast."

— Uwe

Again three parallel simple truths; *you can't help but get better—just not enough time yet*—and *we want success too fast.* These are all related, all integrated into a central theme—that of *time*. The foundation of process is one of time, a quantity that measures duration, one that is absolute, and utterly indifferent to you and I. We can't change time, but we can leverage it and appreciate it. I think the best contemporary work I've ever read in relation to the effects and the dynamics of time is the work of Malcolm Gladwell. In his book *Outliers*, Gladwell coined what came to be known as the "10,000-Hour Rule." By researching eminently successful people in the areas of music, athletics and industry, he found a correlation not to intelligence or ambition, but to *time* on task. The "10,000-Hour Rule" was born. It takes 10,000 hours as a practitioner to reach significant mastery. Elite performers (including Tiger Woods, Bill Gates and even the Beatles) get their time on task—and they get it *early!* 10,000 hours spread out would average some 90 minutes a day over 20 years. Elite performers get it done far, far sooner.

What does this have to do with Uwe's simple truths of *you* **can't help but get better—just not enough time yet**—and **we want success too fast**? I take away a couple of lessons on process here. First, I think about where *I* am in relation to the river of time and the 10,000-hour rule. In my professional practice, I've got my 10,000 hours and tens of thousands more. On the guitar, not only am I way shy of the requisite 10,000 hours, given my age and life expectancy I may never get them! There, I've said it. I'll *never* play as well as Uwe, or Jens or Itzhak Perlman.

I think Uwe is also saying here that some of us want 10,000 hours of mastery from only 1,000 hours invested—that is the rush to success he spoke of. It's really just simple math, we're kidding ourselves, but he does add the comforting thought that no matter where we are on the timeline, we *can* enjoy growth. The icing on the cake is that with more time applied to an instrument, or whatever process we apply ourselves to, we can't help but get better with every minute of time invested. Here's a final note on the concept of "time."

Playing Time is Sacred, Pay Yourself First

> *"You have to say 'this is MY time' each day. Playing time is sacred time. The musicians you respect, they're always playing ... that's why they are so good."*

— *Uwe*

The simplest of simple truths? It's in there, he just said it, *time is sacred*. It only flows in one direction and we don't want to waste it. Here's more from Uwe on time as it relates to process:

"Playing music is the most democratic of things. You cannot buy the ability in the store. You have to put in the time."

"I said before, putting music into your life is about managing distractions and setting boundaries. If you can't find time, make a plan, a schedule for it. Plan for how many hours of sleeping, working, or interacting each day."

"Playing time is your time ... it is sacred time. And we buy everything in life with time, so set aside sacred time. Pay yourself first."

"If you don't take your own time out, you'll always be chasing it and never catching it. Time is the only asset there is. When I travel and perform, I get zero personal time and I have to make up for that when I get back home."

— *Uwe*

Playing time is sacred, pay yourself first! Time for your music, time for your family, your kids, your work, it's a sacred zero-sum entity. It's a fixed amount, and what about time for you? I love the seat back card on airplanes that tell us to "put your own mask on first." Yet, especially in the most important of environments, we always seem to do for others before ourselves. Always. What happens when time runs out? I gave you a "life calculator" earlier ... we only get so many wake-ups. How many do you have left? ***Playing time is sacred, pay yourself first.*** My friend Marshall is fond of saying that on your death bed it's unlikely that you'll be surrounded by co-workers ... and he asks us what advice would the ninety-five-year-old *you* give you right now, today? Take that advice, secure your own mask first. ***Playing time is sacred, pay yourself first.***

The More You Know, the More You Enjoy

> *"People ask me, do they need to learn more moves, more licks. Generally speaking, the more you know the more you enjoy!"*
>
> — *Uwe*

I used to always read novels on airplanes. I travel regularly for business, and at one time

I would habitually consume lots of fiction to absorb time on airplanes and in hotel rooms. I guess my thinking was; *I spend all day thinking about business ... I deserve a break.* But I have to say that as I've matured in my professional practice—as I've become aware of the process—I now find that I almost always read work-related *non*-fiction in that captive time. I'm eager to know more and more about behavioral change, about habit loops, about brain science. You name it, I soak it all up now. And guess what—I have *tons* more fun in what I do to earn a living than ever before. Work the process!

"This is how music works. You learn all of these chess moves and then put them together in a creative way. You don't have to reinvent the wheel every time you come up with a new song."

— *Uwe*

Life is like that too. As with any growth, the development of insight, of experience matters. It matters a lot. Think about the most important "process" on the planet—parenting. I have three daughters, eight years apart from youngest to oldest. Do you think I behaved any differently as a father from the first daughter to the second? Had I learned anything from the first to the third? You bet I had. And shame on me if I hadn't learned and grown. When it came my youngest daughter's turn to bang up one of my vehicles (they all get their turn) I went out to the drive to look at it. My only comment was, *"It's fine, nobody got hurt."* My eldest had witnessed this and asked, "Who are you, and what have you done with my father?" We learn different "moves" over time. We learn what works and when to use the moves—in music and in life.

Uwe is right on; **the more you know, the more you enjoy**—*whatever* it is you apply yourself to. And would you like a bonus simple truth here? My eldest daughter's mentor, Todd Durkin, has a saying; *"If you don't like it, it's because you need it."* Todd is an internationally-known fitness professional and coach and he's referring to specific exercises. If you don't like push ups, it might be that you have some weaknesses in certain muscles of the shoulder ... and that you do in fact *need* push-ups! *If you don't like it, it's because you need it.* I think the same is true of this musical process of studying and mastering licks, scales, positions, theory and everything else I delude myself into thinking I don't deserve to be burdened with. I *do* need it. Thank you, Uwe. Thank you, Todd.

––––––––––

Reduce Variables to Remove Distraction

> *"To play music well, get rid of distractions. It's not your ability to memorize that is in question, it's your ability to shut things out. Go for consistency every time you play. Reduce variables to remove distraction."*
>
> — *Uwe*

"Get rid of distractions." Let's start there. This is the age of what I call the time/technology paradox. I get it—we *need* our electronic companions—but we also need purposeful relief from their presence. Most people I know never turn off their smart phone; from the day they buy it to the day they upgrade. I have coached people that complain of lack of sleep while admitting they were responding to work emails at 2:30 a.m. the previous night. Others feel like they consider it their job to *"drink the waterfall,"* with no excuse NOT to drink the waterfall and no breaks allowed. Most of them receive over 200 emails every day, and guess what? Most people you meet can't pay attention for more that about eighteen seconds. In fact, there is only a 50-50 chance in *any* conversation that either party is listening at any given moment.

I'll bet you've never considered that there are millions of television channels on the planet, with hundreds of millions of hours of programming being broadcast every day. Is it any wonder that every scrap of news is *breaking* news! Is it just me or do we really have to name every little winter storm that blows through? With so many voices vying for our attention, it's a wonder we can even think at all. **Reduce variables to remove distraction.**

There is a cost to all these distractions. I do know we find it hard to care for others at the end of the day. This time/technology paradox has hurt us. Bad. Today's average American college student cares less about others than the same student of less than twenty years ago. Empathy today is way down, and narcissism is way up. If we can't care for others, how can we ever expect to care for our music? Remove the myriad distractions to your process.

Get rid of distractions. **Reduce variables to remove distraction.** Wiser words have never been spoken. Get rid of distractions. Setting up technology-free zones and times is a good start. I've seen it work for my clients. Any effort to reduce variables pays dividends as well. I know this because I've used the technique for myself. One example is, I have a "uniform" that I wear when I speak professionally. I have several sets of the same pants and shirts that I take wherever I travel. A mentor showed me this by example decades ago, and it still reduces variables and therefore distractions for me decades later. I never have to think about wardrobe, or about packing. The Kruger Brothers also deploy the same strategy. They always perform with the same amps, the same microphones, the same carpet, and they too wear the same uniform for every show.

There are never-ending distractions competing for your attention today, so go set some boundaries now. In 1966 the culture cry made famous by Timothy Leary was to "turn on & tune in." I think the far more relevant phrase today might be to just turn off and tune up. Take a look at your life. Find out where and how you can turn off the noise. Write it down now in your journal. Look to reduce process variables in every part of your life; your music, your work, your family. The possibilities are endless, the rewards unlimited.

Adopt process, not practice. A *learning* process is really what we've been discussing. *Learning*; to acquire knowledge or skill by study, instruction or experience. Uwe is very pragmatic when it comes to learning. He tells it like it is, not as I might wish it would be.

Let's study this idea of a learning platform, and several more succinct simple truths.

———————

You Need It, You Learn It

> *"When you need it, you learn it ... whether a child learning to brush their teeth, or you learning a simple 'G' scale."*

> *"If you want to become a virtuoso, there is a school for that. Attend that school and you will become a virtuoso. But will that make you happy? Is that what you need?"*

> *"Be happy with what you can do, because if you're not happy you have no chance of ever learning. It's only when you relax and let go that you ever learn something."*

— *Uwe*

The common theme here, the unifying thread that precariously holds the learning process together, is *you*. Your wants and needs. When *you need it, you learn it.* Will something make *you* happy? Is it what you need, and can you relax and let go in order to learn something? Yes, it is all about you after all!

Uwe's approach to the learning process is obviously adult-centered. I'm not saying he couldn't teach a child; I'm saying that the vast majority of his practice and his guidance reflect self-directed, task-centered observations. It's a delicate balance, but Uwe has help for you; in fact, get ready for a lesson.

"Most of the time, we just open a book with tablatures and we play and it's sort of like, yeah, that's good ... next song. We can't really play it well yet, but we think it will be OK next time. So we turn to the next page, to the next song, and do it all over again—and in the end we haven't played a single note of real music!"

"Nowadays we have Pandora, Spotify or an iPod on shuffle and we don't listen in depth anymore ... it's detrimental to a musical practice. Use technology to record, to give you feedback. Let it work for you."

"With learning a new song, put your iPod on 'repeat' and listen to it phrase by phrase ... listen to it until you can sing it. Once you can sing it, then there's no problem picking up the instrument and playing along."

"In learning songs, you name things to be able to put them in an understandable context ... a 'brush,' a 'hit,' 'hammer-on' or 'pull-off.' We do it to connect semantic thought with the physical sensations of playing."

"Learn all the songs that the people you love already know. Learn to play 'Happy Birthday,' or the 'National Anthem.' Learn your daddy's or your brother's or your husband's or wife's favorite song. That's what we do and why we learn—to entertain other people!"

— Uwe

Wow, nice lesson—*you need it, you learn it*!

1. Immerse yourself in a song

2. Learn it—say it—sing it—play it

3. Let the instrument fill in after you learn

4. If you can name it, you can claim it

5. Learn the songs that "they" love

Learn to Ask

"One of the most powerful new rules of engagement in any part of life is to learn to ask instead of tell."

— *Don*

In every area of my professional practice, learning to *ask* is part of it. Life is too complex to think we always have the answer. And asking is a very important part of any learning process—that of learning from others. Eleanor Roosevelt is quoted as saying, "Learn from the mistakes of others. You can't live long enough to make them all yourself." Aint that the truth! I've made lots of mistakes in my life, and in my 30's I finally grew up enough to be capable of learning from others. In order to learn from others, two things have to happen; you have to first be comfortable being the "newbie," and second, you have to grow up and *learn to ask*. I grew up in Detroit, but in my 30's took up trail riding on horseback. I now live on seventeen acres and over the last fifteen to twenty years have owned and stabled horses at home that my daughters learned to ride and show. Trust me, this city kid learned to ask—a lot. Likewise, I took up basketball in my 30's, and at forty-five started playing soccer two to three times a week. I have learned how to ask—and it's perhaps the best way to accelerate the learning process.

Uwe too has some very distinct observations around asking and learning from others. In fact, I'd like to start another "lesson" for you, a lesson on learning, with a quote from a conversation Uwe had with my middle daughter Kelly. The Kruger Brothers had played "The Ark" here in Ann Arbor and stayed at our house. While sitting out in the courtyard on a summer morning, Uwe said to my daughter: "Kelly, do you know what I like so much about your dad? He's not always trying to show me how good he is."

That very personal comment was just the tip of the iceberg when it came to Uwe on learning from others:

> *"My mom used to tell me, sit next to the smartest kid in class and you'll learn the most."*
>
> *"When I asked my Uncle about guitar lessons, he said everybody in the world knows something about music that you don't, and if you learn to ask the right questions, they can teach you."*
>
> *"Don, find the one thing you can extract from another and ask politely enough so that you can actually learn it ... something will rub off."*

"In learning music, as with almost anything else, get close to someone who is much better than you are and pay attention."

"The only way I learned how to play guitar was by always playing with someone better than me and not being afraid of it."

"Try to learn things you've never tried before. You may not like it, but you will know for certain you don't like it."

"Sometimes it's best not to force it ... it's letting go of the wanting that makes learning happen."

"Always remember—if you're the biggest fish in the tank, you're never going to have fun—you're just going to end up eating everyone else!"

— *Uwe*

Another heck of a lesson: **learn to ask**:

1. It's OK to show what you *don't* know

2. Get close to the best

3. Ask politely

4. Pay attention

5. Let go of fear and ego

The heart of that lesson is *asking*. Ask the right questions—ask politely—ask for help. And for me, asking—balancing empathy over ego—has been the foundation of every one of my life's critical decisions (at least all the *good* ones). Swapping ego for empathy in asking Colleen if she wanted to get married thirty-five years ago; asking a friend to arrange for Marshall Goldsmith to be on my thesis review board; breaking bread on a Sunday morning in the Kruger's Wilkesboro studio and asking Uwe if I might write up the very work you're reading now. *Asking* takes only subordination of ego to empathy, it costs nothing and gives back *so* much. Asking unlocks the magic of learning from others and ignites the learning process.

Every Note is Equal

> **"Every note is equal. Give each one its due. On any instrument, every note is a unique piece of art. Not a single note—or rest—is unimportant."**

— *Uwe*

My reflection here is to tell myself, the process applies to me too—*don't be so lazy, Don!* Don't skip over a passage because it's hard to play. Have you ever done this? Do you ever spend a great deal of time and energy figuring out how to work *around* the tough part of a song, or a tough part of life? We're better off putting that same energy into mastering the passage rather than avoiding it. When I take the path of least resistance, the passage either trips me up (in the same place every time), or it never quite sounds as it should, even if I'm able to play through it. I have to admit too that I've spent significant amounts of personal energy over the years working around difficult *people* in my life too. That never ends well. **Every note is equal**. Skip the work-around and give every note, every moment its due.

Let's reconsider this group of simple truths regarding *the process* of learning; the *way* of growth from beginner to expert:

- **Adopt Process, Not Practice**
- **Can't Help but Get Better**
- **Just Not Enough Time Yet**
- **We Want Success Too Fast**
- **Playing Time is Sacred, Pay Yourself First**
- **The More You Know, the More You Enjoy**
- **If You Don't Like It, It's Because You Need It**
- **Reduce Variables to Remove Distraction**

- *You Need It, You Learn It*
- *Learn to Ask*
- *Every Note is Equal*

Wow, what a list! Before we move on to simple truths about *your* personal path, your life's journey, I'll have Uwe close with a very profound final observation on the learning process.

> *"The process of learning the guitar is like a 1,500 piece puzzle. In the beginning, it takes days and days and you don't see anything, and then finally the picture comes together and it gets easier and easier the further you go."*
>
> — *Uwe*

It's Your Path

Let's take a breath for a minute. Breathing is a two-for-one you know, it allows a pause for thinking and reflection, and it also provides all the oxygen your brain is going to need for this treatise on one's path—one's journey. You might want to take a couple of deep breaths right now.

"Before you can play as well as Doc Watson, first you have to be as good a man as Doc Watson."

— Uwe

How's that for a powerful opener? We've spoken of a musician's practice and of the learning process, but now it gets *personal*. We are all on our own personal *path* in this practice of music. Alone. One size does not fit all. The path is ours alone. Sometimes we're on it blind; sometimes we're moving with light, purpose and intention. My path is different from yours, different from Uwe's— and neither Uwe nor I are better or worse for that variance. Let this be the first simple truth in this discussion of your path.

It's Your Path

"Don, don't worry how you come across or what the world thinks ... it's your path. As musicians, we should be the last ones to care."

— Uwe

It's your path. What *I* am doing, including my music, is *my* path, not Uwe's, not my brother's, not my friend's, my wife's or my kids' path. It is distinctly mine. In discussions such as these, I always think of Gandhi's words:

*"Your beliefs become your thoughts
your thoughts become your words
your words become your actions
your actions become your habits
your habits become your values
your values become your destiny."*

— *Mahatma Gandhi*

In my mind, this ultimate *destiny* is *my* path in life, and especially as it relates to music I take comfort in some more of Uwe's words on the subject.

"We all have a path—and if you're on the same path with another, how important is it really to be ahead or behind? Not at all."

"Playing an instrument can sometimes work against self-esteem. If you play a song and it might not be as good as what she just played, does it become a competition? Does that make you a worse person than her? Do you believe that?"

"You're just like me or anyone else in the room, so give it your all, enjoy and embrace your music."

— *Uwe*

It's your path. How much of our lives do we spend comparing other's paths, judging other's paths, tending other's paths, and even making over our paths in the likeness of another? Of late, I often hear a cute phrase in reference to minding one's own business; "not my monkey, not my zoo." I think I'll just restate that to be "not my path," and to dedicate myself ... to *my* path. That doesn't mean I will be blind to the paths of others. In fact, I'd like to tell you about my path in life and you can decide for yourself.

You will note on the spine of this book a very stylized character just like the one you see here. This character is one of happiness, with a bit of luck or good fortune in there as well. A character or "chop" such as this often represents one's identity or, at least, a personal philosophy. My philosophy of life and work—and my music—is a path of happiness. Happiness for myself, and more importantly what I can contribute to the happiness of others. My path, or dharma, is to "help people with people"—to both help maximize their outcomes, and in the end, to help them feel good about it. In fact, I've written a song entitled, *The Gift You Can Never Repay*. Everything about my path, in music as in life, is currently shaped around the giving of gifts that can never be repaid. **It's your path.**

Reflecting upon all of the interviews, lessons and personal conversations with Uwe regarding one's path, just a few words will float to the top for you. Take a look, this first one's impact grew out of only one powerful insight.

Learn the Songs You Know

"Learn the songs you know, because for that you don't need a teacher."
— *Uwe*

Don't you love it when the obvious finally becomes apparent? Even if you've never before played an instrument, you already know lots of songs. Most of us know hundreds —if not *thousands* of songs. We can't yet play them, but we know them and can easily recall them via cues associated with melody, title and lyric. Most of them we learned early in life (while perhaps struggling to absorb our studies I might add). Why did the songs stick? There are a couple of reasons. We learned most of them due to the powerful perfecta of repetition and connection. We heard them over and over again, and we usually had very strong emotions associated with them in one way or another. And we also remember the early songs perhaps because there was more available real estate "upstairs" back then. And maybe more importantly, the older we get, the less repetition we get to establish connections between the song and our current emotional streams.

So, what is the point with "*learn the songs you know*"? Uwe intuitively takes advantage of what is already there to accelerate the development process. You know the songs; they are already connected to strong personal emotions within you. Now all you have to do is insert an instrument. Jump-start the process. Start off by learning the ones you already know—and the bonus is you won't need a teacher—you teach it to yourself. How simple that is, and how obvious now that it's been pointed out. And, what a great way to get high-value time on task too! Before you lose the old song titles that are swimming in your head right now, the ones you know but don't yet play, take a minute for your journal here to write down three or four (or more) that you know—that you want to learn.

Play What Has Stuck

"Just play what has stuck in your mind ... learn all the songs you heard and loved when you were a teenager, all the songs you heard and sang when you first fell in love."

— Uwe

Gosh, the simplicity of this variation on the same theme—just **play what has stuck.** For me it's quite a mix; *My Girl, The Thrill Is Gone, I'm Satisfied, Truckin', Ripple, Crazy, Summertime, Okie From Muskogee, Mi Ultimo Fracaso, I Wanna Be Around, Blackbird. The Temptations, BB King, Mississippi John Hurt, The Dead, Willie Nelson, Doc Watson, Merle Haggard, El Trio Los Panchos, Tony Bennett, The Beatles*—to name only a few of what's rolling around in my brain bucket. As I mentioned before, most of us have literally thousands of songs that have "stuck" to one degree or another. What I've realized is that these songs make up the trailhead, the beginnings of my musical path. I already play many of these songs, but not all. Why not, and what about you? What has *stuck* for you? What artists, and what songs in particular have stuck? I believe this is so important that I ask you to right now go to the journaling pages. Start a couple of pages with "**play what has stuck**" written at the top—and write down all of the many titles and artists that come to mind—the ones that have stuck to you! Invite a friend to join you to brainstorm the ones that stuck. I'll be here waiting for you when you're done.

———

Music Our Parents Played

"What each of us believes is right or wrong about music has a lot to do with the music our parents played ... what we listened to when we were kids."

"When I was little, we had a big hay field outside the house ... I'd get asthma attacks so that I had to stay inside the house a lot ... one time when my dad was on a trip, I asked my mom if she could teach me how to play the guitar. She taught me seven chords in a week (my fingers were bleeding!) and when my dad came home I played him a song and he sat there crying. My heart was never so full."

— Uwe

Music our parents played—and "who matters to you." With Uwe and Jens it's very obvious that their mother and father meant a great deal to them. Their music is in many ways a tribute to them. This isn't the case for everyone, but what Uwe is asking is who specifically had that influence upon you, and what music did you hear them playing when you were growing up? My parents had a big stereo system that my father had built from a Radio Shack kit. I vividly remember them listening to soundtrack LPs of musicals (Carousel, The Sound Of Music, Oklahoma), and to Eddy Arnold, Perry Como, Dean Martin and lots of Scottish singers and pipe and drum recordings.

In thinking back, it seems mostly my mom's influence on the selections that we heard —all of the romantic ballads of Eddy, Perry and Dean. Come to think of it, my mom's side of the family was the musical side. Growing up, on holidays we would mostly gather with her side's relatives at our house, her brother's house or her sister's house, and every one of those gatherings ended with us kids and cousins playing recitals. We would pass around lyric sheets and sing Christmas carols together to help digest the holiday meal. The Scottish musical influence came from both sides, my mother and father's.

Uwe then asks about who matters to us. He spoke of the impact of his father's emotional response to his own music, and I'm willing to bet that Doc Watson's approval meant and still means a great deal to Uwe. He now asks who matters to us. I can say just as strongly now that the opinions and involvement of my parents and family mattered way back. Now my wife and daughters matter, some of my friends. Uwe, Jens and Joel have come to matter to me as well, and let me share a side story. Maynard Holbrook, a fabulous singer and very close friend to the Kruger brothers, has also come to matter to me. During musical academy performance night, I performed a song I'd written for my daughter's wedding. For this performance, I also arranged it for banjo, bass and cello and sang it with Jean Hatmaker of the Kontras Quartet. Afterwards Maynard sought me out and said through smiling eyes—*"that song 'He's the One' was your song wasn't it? It was absolutely wonderful!"* I was stunned in the realization of how much *he* mattered to me. At another Academy performance to mark the passing of Merle Haggard, I dedicated his song, "Today I Started Loving You Again," to Maynard and his love for all the sad old songs he sings. Afterwards he again sought me out to give a thumbs up and tell me *"Merle woulda been proud."* I only see Maynard once a year, but yes, Maynard matters to me. Who matters to you? What did your parents used to play? Go now to the journaling pages to write down these musical landmarks on your path. *Music our parents played—tell me, who matters to you*? Again, I'll be waiting, and when you get back we'll tackle our path's built-in GPS ... your *heart.*

Without Heart is Unforgivable

"Beethoven once said, 'to play a mistake is human, to play without heart is unforgivable.' Perfect comes from repetition, but play comes from the heart!"

— *Uwe*

To *play* **without heart is unforgivable**. Play comes from the heart—a truth so simple it can become cliché. Don't let it. I think I did for a long time. I grew up in an era of male role models the likes of John Wayne or Clint Eastwood—not the most emotive of heroes. I even have a coffee cup with a picture of John Wayne on it with the quote, "Talk low, talk slow and don't say too much." We were expected to hide our feelings, to *hide* our hearts. Add in a dour Scottish cultural influence in which the watchwords are "shut your gob and do your job"—it's a wonder I can find my heart at all.

Over the last decade or so though, I've been able to drop the facades a little, to try and ignore the alleged safety of the walls we put up to protect ourselves. The sad thing is, sometimes everybody has his or her walls up to the point where there's almost no human contact at all. Perhaps it's safe, but it's cold as heck. Music plays a big part in tearing down those walls for me. And, guess what? The more I wear my heart on my sleeve instead of hiding it, the more others do as well. You want a better world, *you* go first ... the ultimate gift that can never be repaid.

Do What is Natural for You

> *"Don, you don't have to always explain why you like a song—just do what is natural for you."*
> — Uwe

Do what comes natural. My discussion with Uwe on this put a new twist on some long held beliefs for me. I've always told others, "follow your gifts, and do what comes easy." I mentioned my girls growing up and wondering what to study for their B.A. I always said "go with easy, you'll get great grades and have fun at the same time." Uwe agreed with the idea of following one's gifts, but changed my thinking with the idea that what feels natural may not necessarily be easy (much the same as "simple but not easy."). Follow your gifts, go with what feels natural ... spontaneous, unaffected, genuine, innate, instinctive, legitimate. There's a difference. Easy can often be taken for granted. Easy can make for lazy. Natural makes for fully heartfelt. Our friend Maynard told me one time, "My wife would always ask me, why do you sing all those *sad* songs? And I said, cause I *like* 'em!" Sad comes natural for Maynard Holbrook. Listen to him sing sometime and you'll know exactly what I mean by *natural*. **Do what is natural for you**. That in fact is *your* path.

I want to add something here that I've learned over the last couple of years too: what's in our hearts and what is natural for us at any given point on the path is not static. It's dynamic, and I'll add a related truth of my own; *everything ends.* My father passed away two years ago; my mother now suffers from Alzheimer's; last year I ended what had been a twenty-five-year business affiliation; and Colleen and I are now officially empty nesters. These changes are natural. Change within our musical paths is natural—*everything ends* sooner or later—and that's OK! Uwe agrees:

> **"A song has a life for you too. Some mature and age well. Others die!"**
>
> — *Uwe*

Your path; a period of travel—a passage from one stage to another. It's time now to bring our discussion of our path and indeed our practice to a close. Let's do that with a solid barrage of appropriate Uwe-isms:

"Inner rhythm is something that guides all of our lives. Do your own thing and find your audience!"

"The most beautiful songs and acts come when the words and melodies are guided by our heart."

"Play with warmth and humanity. Lose all arrogance and hostility, just put yourself into your music."

"If we only try to please other people, to do stuff that makes us look good in others' eyes, that makes us a bootlegger."

"Let your life and music touch people simply because it touches you."

"If freedom's just another word for nothing left to lose, then the first thing to lose is the fear of what other people think of you."

"Johnny Cash once told me: 'If you go follow somebody, nobody will follow you—they'll just follow that somebody too.'"

— *Uwe*

Your practice—the process—your path. What a journey this has been! Just within this movement alone we've absorbed another twenty-one powerfully simple truths, extracted from dozens of succinct conversational excerpts. I think we need a break right now. Any rest is equal to any note. I've had readers over the years tell me they ended up spending hours in a single sitting traveling from start to finish in reading my work; that they were unable to put it down until done. Take a pause *now* though. Step away from the book. Let it rest. Go play some music, consider your practice of music and life. Then when you're ready, open your heart to the capacity to **create***!*

Third Movement

CREATE

Moments You Can't Rehearse

Another one of my pastimes is cooking. The game there, like in music, is to have a vision of a flavor in my head—and then try to recreate that in a pot!

First comes a picture, a vision of what you want. It doesn't have to be complex, it just evokes an interval; a color; an emotion. That is what we all then share each time we create it with an audience.

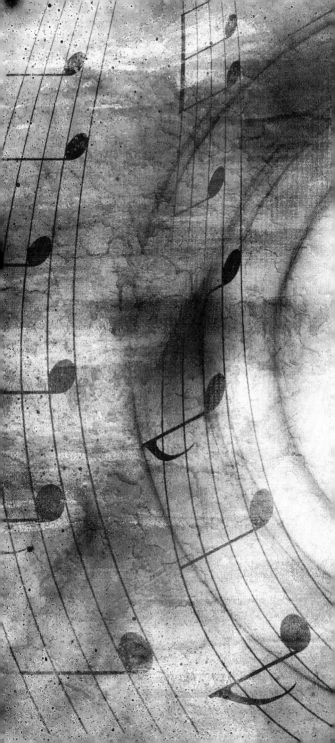

Sometimes it's best not to force it ... sometimes it's letting go of the wanting that makes things happen!

I appreciate mountain music because just five words can mean so much. I've always thought that was much more alluring.

The title sets the stage.

Jens and I have a saying, "music starts happening when it starts to become boring." When your brain starts to do things on its own to get out of boredom— that is when creativity starts.

There is a good song for almost everything you can imagine … and it's your job to find them. That is creativity at work.

I only write a song when I have to; otherwise I just want to find a good song.

It's a question of "Do I like the world that these people paint for me? Do I want to be a part of that world?"

Once you find the right song and set your intention, you don't have much choice anymore.

og, pa
ng ho
ention
nd in
estina

Think about
Blackbird.
You can't do
that better.
Ever. Period.

Play—Practice—Create. Next in line in Uwe's taxonomy of music and life is the word "create." Much as with "play" he seems to light up at the very thought of almost any application of the word "create." I am seeing a pattern emerging here too. "Play" like a *child.* A *glad* taking of one's responsibility for one's "practice." And in this movement, a *joyful* desire to "create" in every corner of life. Guess what? *This enthusiasm matters!*

Enthusiasm is Power

"Don't kid yourself, enthusiasm is power!"

— *Don*

I'm starting this movement with a truth of my own. *Enthusiasm is power.* While not built upon Uwe's words, I see it in his actions. I have seen the truth evident in most every rub of his life against that of others. *Enthusiasm is power.* I also see it in traditional achievement metrics that might be applied to Uwe's work: the symmetry of his lyrics, the impact of his storytelling and the colorful mastery of his instrument. Uwe is as creative—and as enthusiastic—as they come. It was while writing this book that I discovered the power of one's enthusiasm —and our capacity to actually generate and direct that enthusiasm.

What first woke me up to the idea was one writer's blog that described just how much her creativity *and* productivity rose while writing sections she was excited about, and how it also dropped like a rock in the sections she deemed more mundane and less interesting. Given five years with Uwe, I'll go one step further—we can *generate* that enthusiasm. We can bring it to the task—with purpose, and on purpose. I've discovered that when I listen to my Kruger Brothers station on Pandora *before* I sit down to write, my productivity (the number of words per hour) and the quality of my words (based on my own post-assessment of them) go up dramatically. I do this intentionally now, I amp up my own enthusiasm prior to writing. I'm aware of it, too. I know I'm doing it when I do it—and it still works! The quality and quantity of my output in writing this book accelerates even more when I sit down with my instrument and *play* music beforehand. It aint magic, but if it is, it's because I *made* it so!

I'm beginning this movement with this truth because I want you to consider and remember that *you* control that capacity to create. It doesn't reside within the activity —*you* bring it to the activity. This applies everywhere, not just within the creative process. **Enthusiasm is power.** Don't be caught without it! *Create*. Let's set our foundation now—enthusiastically—with an operational definition:

Create: *to cause to come into being; from idea to existence; to perform for the first time; by composition or interpretation, by design or display; to produce using imagination and talent; to build, conceive, construct or discover.*

There is a dichotomy of creation in music that is unique and doesn't apply to other art forms. Some would have you believe that the creative process is confined to composing and writing original work. Period. Yet, I've discovered with Uwe that creation takes place not just within original composition, but within interpretation as well. Probably the ultimate evidence of this dichotomy is found in "Somewhere Over the Rainbow." You've seen "The Wizard of Oz," and you've heard the classic rendition by Judy Garland. Now, go to YouTube and listen to the song's interpretation by a Hawaiian named Israel "Iz" Kamakawiwoʻole. Check it out! No one can refute the possibility of creation within interpretation *after* they hear it. No one.

So consider this contrast then in our definition of "by design or display, composition or interpretation." With dozens of quotes and simple truths that govern creation and creativity, I'll divide our discussion using that final pairing—*composition* versus *interpre-*

tation. The former is targeted to the creation of original work, the latter in support of our efforts to present the music of others. Are you ready?

———

Composition: *the creation of original work.*

First Comes a Picture

"First comes a picture, a vision of what you want. It doesn't have to be complex, it just evokes an interval, a color, an emotion— what we all then share with an audience."

"Another one of my pastimes is cooking. The game there, like in music, is to have a vision of a flavor in my head and then try to recreate that in a pot!"

— *Uwe*

First comes a picture. Uwe is a *very* visual guy, especially in such an auditory business. I've shared several of our conversations with you; "Don, what do you *see*?"; "Every key has a different *color*"; "a *vision* of what you want"; "a *vision* of a flavor." Part of my studies of the applied behavioral sciences includes a concept called Neuro-Linguistic Programming, or NLP. NLP helps to explain how each of us prefers to take in, process and communicate information. There are four distinct "systems" in NLP: visual, auditory, kinesthetic and digital. When you have a conversation with someone and they prefer a visual representation system you'll hear words like we do from Uwe; "see," "look," "watch," "vision," "color." If the individual prefers an auditory system of processing the world as I do, you might repeatedly hear words such as "listen," "hear," "sounds good" or "sounds like" to communicate their perspective. Now, I'm not going any further into NLP than that, but you may Google it to find out more. I only bring it up in response to a question that has been nagging at the back of my mind; is Uwe's use of such terms just coincidental to a more visual preference—or *is the creative process itself visually related*, for *all* of us, regardless of whether we're visual, auditory, kinesthetic or digital in preference? Here is what I found out.

According to the latest brain science, reality and imagination seem to flow inversely along the same paths within our brains, across what they call our "mental workspace." Visual information that your eyes take in flows from the bottom up across the brain's lobes, and images that you imagine travel top down, but across that same area. This "flow" I'm talking about refers to the general direction of electrical signaling within our brains—the way the current moves. I believe there really could be a *visual* correlation then to the creative process; a foundation of imagining, or forming an image in our mind's eye (a "vision" in Uwe's words) of things that cannot yet be perceived through any of our senses. Perhaps creativity begins visually, whether we're aware of it or not.

First comes a picture. What a profound statement. And, those of us with a different style preference might want to start exploring that "visual" side of life. In fact, as a kinesthetic and auditory person that tends to process information via feelings and sounds, I think I'm actually limiting my own creative potential. Remember what Uwe told me early on? *"Don, discover what you see and the song is yours."*

Moments You Can't Rehearse

"Creation is one of the moments you can't rehearse. It's scary even."
— *Uwe*

We just finished talking about the brain science of creation. Now we have the yin to the yang: creation not as science, but as magical, mystical, even inexplicable. Uwe isn't the only one to acknowledge the unanswerable when it comes to composition.

"I pick up the pen and God moves it."

— *Hank Williams*

"The songs are there...just waiting for someone to write them down. If I didn't do it, someone else would."

— *Bob Dylan*

"If I need a melody, I pluck it out of the air."

— *Willie Nelson*

"Some days it gets very, very spooky."

— *Lionel Richie*

"I wrote 'If I Needed You' in my sleep."

— *Townes Van Zandt*

"Even the best gardener can't make a single flower."

— *Robert Wyatt*

Moments you can't rehearse. When it comes down to it, sometimes there are no definitive answers, only perspectives. This is an era of ambiguity. The ability to live and work with ambiguity is a much sought after competency today. The paradigm of always having to have all the answers is a dying one. The same is true with creativity. Most songwriters can't differentiate a "hit" until after the fact. Sometimes we can't predict and control the process of original or interpretive creation any more than we can control the weather. ***Moments you can't rehearse.*** We can only prepare for them and maybe take full advantage when they do come.

Letting Go Makes It Happen

> **"Sometimes it's best not to force it. At times, the letting go makes it happen."**
>
> — *Uwe*

This statement about the creative process really does it for me. Thank you for the new lens on it, Uwe. ***Letting go makes it happen.*** In many ways I am in the *letting go* business. I help people with people—and this almost invariably means helping people to do something differently in their lives in order to be more effective with others. To let go of one thing and pick up on another. Heck, I wrote a book entitled "What Got You Here Won't Get You There—in Sales," the implication being what got you *here* will get you *here*, meaning more of the same. Generally, if you want to get "there," to create anew, it's going to take letting go of something in your life to make room for the new. I hadn't before considered it a process of creation. I now do.

Let's add the how-to. It's very simple, very succinct. It's just a two-syllable imperative: *time's up!* Letting go is usually so difficult for us because for the most part we don't *have* to let go. It's a choice—a logical, positive choice—but a choice nonetheless. We don't *have* to let go and there are usually lots of reasons to stay in our current comfort zone. In essence, we usually really want to hold on for a just a little while longer, to not let go. And we hold on as years go by. Sometimes a lifetime will go by without letting go. What is the mantra to more effective creativity? *"Time's up!"* Time is up for letting go of wanting something—without doing something about it. Time is up for letting go of fear—without facing it. Time is up in letting go of blind certainty—without listening to another perspective. **Letting go makes it happen**. Let go now.

So how *do* we let go? Two words; *gratitude* and *separation*. Letting go with a grateful heart, not with sadness, but a thankful appreciation for what we are letting go of. Then, consciously creating the needed separation from the now state. That might include separation from people, places, behaviors, or from whatever triggers give us just more of the same. **Letting go makes it happen.** *Time's up!*

———————

Five Words Can Mean So Much

"I appreciate mountain music because five words can mean so much. I've always thought that was much more alluring. I like brevity, I like it straightforward. Longer compositions can lose you—but some, like 'The Edmund Fitzgerald' hold me ... the lyrics create a world not just that I like, but that I want to stay in and explore!"

— *Uwe*

Five words can mean so much: Hemmingway, not Faulkner. Gotcha Uwe. If you recall, Uwe's approach to playing technique also advocates less, not more. Why not his approach to creativity? Brevity is his preference, but not an absolute as evidenced by his quote about "The Edmund Fitzgerald" (he really lit up when he talked about it). I have always loved reading Hemmingway versus Faulkner, but *both* received the Nobel Prize for literature. I love the simple, direct songs of Hank Williams, but I also love "El Paso" or "Gentle on My Mind." William Faulkner, according to the *Guinness Book of World Records*, holds the honor of having written the longest sentence in published literature. On the other hand, Hemmingway's writing philosophy can be summed up in fourteen words. "Write the best story you can, and write it as straight as you can." In the end, Uwe sides with Hemingway. ***Five words can mean so much.***

Why do we sometimes err on the Faulkner side? A couple of reasons probably. I imagine a lifetime of academic programming plays a part. We are always working towards page count or word count, and the higher your education, the more it comes into play. Some of us then develop a passive voice that adds words, but subtracts impact. We might even underestimate our audience at times too. ***Five words can mean so much:*** "Last Thing On My Mind," "All You Need Is Love," "I Can't Get No Satisfaction." Can you think of your five-word favorites?

This may be only indirectly related, but I am smiling right now as I recall Jens Kruger asking a question after raising the roof with a song he had just played on the banjo. He laughed deeply and asked the audience, *"Too many notes? I always worry about too many notes."* Never too many notes from you Jens, but too many words from most of us.

Five words can mean so much. It really comes down to respecting the listener to find that balance between brevity and clarity. Respect the listener, as you would have them "do unto you." I've been known to be that guy that keeps up a conversation that should be done, just because *I'm* having so much fun. I even tell people all the time—*"Don't sell past the close."* Don't be that guy. **Five words can mean so much.** Thank you Uwe.

Bored is OK!

> **"Jens and I have a saying: 'music starts happening when the music starts to become boring.' When you listen to it and play it so many times you become bored ... that's when your brain starts doing things on its own, to get out of the boredom. Creativity kicks in with boredom. Bored is OK!"**
>
> — *Uwe*

Man, again with the obvious becoming apparent. ***Bored is OK****!* Examples are everywhere. The child that invents her own game (or her own best friend) when no one else is around; the million-dollar patent born when least expected; heck, even Newton's "discovery" of gravity just sitting under a tree! From discussing this quote with Uwe, I know he and Jens have performed certain songs or compositions so many times, in so many cities, on so many stages that they can't help but become bored during a given performance, regardless of how much they *love* the piece! I'm pretty sure it might happen with several songs, even the ones they've written, and especially the ones that every audience wants to hear every show. What's a musician to do?

Bored is OK. Allowing for boredom, even embracing and encouraging it makes this a better world. But sometimes we don't let it happen. Think about it. Our kids get bored easily; they start making noise, and what do we do? We put video screens in every car's seatback. A movie grabs their attention for 120 minutes—and we get two hours of peace and quiet in the front seat. Another example would be the explosion of organized sports for those same children. We program, organize and dictate every one of our sons' and daughters' training sessions, practices, games and tournaments. They're safe, protected, and programmed to a predictable path. But they own nothing for themselves. They create nothing, in fact—they might even *really* dislike that very sport that you and they are dedicating so much time to. ***Bored is OK.***

And, what about you? Do you embrace boredom for yourself? During the book's first movement on "play" we discussed what I call our time/technology paradox. What we admittedly *need* to be competitive today— iPhones, laptops and the internet—is also killing our creativity. My middle daughter calls it *"watching cat videos."* We are never without these electronic distractions either. We always have important, or at least urgent notifications coming in from our electronics. It keeps us in our conscious, focused, deliberate brains—and rarely allows the unconscious to take over. Every ding and buzz is an electronic interruption. A manufactured distraction that doesn't allow getting "stuck."

Uwe and Jens get stuck. They *anticipate* getting stuck, getting bored. And then they let their unconscious take over to get them *un*stuck. Those are the shows where the roof is raised and the barn doors get blown off. **Bored is OK.** Get stuck; turn off the tech; confine yourself to quarters and let boredom set in. Let the conscious you turn off. Let your subconscious turn on!

The Title Sets the Stage

> *"The title sets the stage. A good title puts a listener on a journey, and the best titles will put you in the right mood to perform it every time too!*
>
> — *Uwe*

The title sets the stage. A song's title—its distinctive name. The word "title" is simply defined, and is synonymous with the word "name" in any dictionary. A song's title is its label, what first distinguishes it from another. Uwe told me how important it is to song writing, to the performer and to the listener, and like most of his guidance it sent me off in search of more. The title; the name. I believe it was Shakespeare through his character Juliet that coined the phrase, *"What's in a name?"* A great deal it turns out.

For all of us, self-representation, our personal connection to our own names, begins in the first year of life. It rises above all other noise across a crowded room for us, and activates our brains in a way nothing else can. When our brains activate, chemicals are released and the effect becomes physiological. All from a word, or set of words, a journey begins. Think of the "titles" of some songs that stuck to you—and the journey you begin just reading them.

"Yesterday" / "Stairway to Heaven" / "My Way" / "Blue Moon of Kentucky" / "Mojo" / "Carolina in The Fall" / "Four Seasons"

Titles and titling don't belong only to songs, think of books, movies, paintings:

"Casablanca" / "Rocky" / "Star Wars" / "The Old Man and the Sea" / "100 Years of Solitude" / "1984" / "The Bible" / "The Quran" / "The Mona Lisa" / "The Last Supper" / "American Gothic"

The title sets the stage. Just a few syllables can send us on a very distinct journey. Your favorites might be different from mine depending on our ages, families, religions, or sum total existence. But some titles, some names can reach out and touch us over decades, or over centuries. The title establishes the art—before we experience the art. And once it's done, it's done. The movie "Casablanca" was going to be titled "Everybody Comes to Rick's." "Annie Hall" almost ended up "Anhedonia" and "Captain America" had a working title of "Frostbite." Different titles create different journeys, or at the very least different expectations of the journey to come.

The most recent book I wrote for McGraw-Hill publishing is a journey of leadership. It's a journey of global research into what our people want us to know, and what they want us to do in leading them. I was very sure I wanted to title it "Return on Leadership" or "Capacity Without Headcount." But, my editor and publisher stuck to their perspective and we went back and forth for a fair amount of time. The result? We ended up with "Bring Out the Best in Every Employee." What a great brand—*bring out the best*! I'm fortunate to have had people around me that stuck to their ideas, and to have had the ability to listen to them.

The title sets the stage—for the performer, and for the listener. My takeaway? The title is the one part of the creative journey where we do well to *invite others into the process*. We're only half of the equation. Would "Casablanca" be a classic today if it had been titled "Everybody Comes to Rick's?" I don't know, maybe. But, I'll say it again—the title establishes the art before we experience the art. The name before the experience. It is often the art's first impression upon others. We only get that one shot at a first impression. In fact, my dad wanted to name me "Angus" (*a guid Scot's name*), and I thank my mom for nixing that one. The title, the *name*, sets the stage. Make it a good one. Make it the right one.

Repeat a Melodic Pattern

> **"Repeat a melodic pattern over and over and see where it takes you, Don."**
>
> *— Uwe*

This one took me to the giving of a gift that can never be repaid. Uwe first told me this during the first Kruger Brothers' Academy back in 2012. What a great weekend! There were four other guitar players with Uwe and I in their Wilkesboro studio for the entire weekend (now it's capped at twenty-five guitarists). We'd been taking turns in the "hot seat" and we started discussing writing songs.

Repeat a melodic pattern Uwe said, and he showed us a simple descending pattern in the key of G. It was almost an off-hand comment, a throw away. But, I realize now he was also building on what we've discussed around boredom as a creative catalyst. The repetition of patterns is central to any song and this one gave me the foundation for the one I then wrote for my oldest daughter on the occasion of her wedding. That pattern came first. While continuing to play it, I not only found a vision for the melody, but for the words too! I ended up emailing her and asked why her fiancé was "the one." It was her answers to that question that then built the lyrics to lay on top of the melody.

Repeat a melodic pattern. Perhaps the truth should read, *find* a melodic pattern. I'd begun writing other songs, some of them through this process of starting with a melodic pattern. The last one came, oddly enough, from nature. We have a courtyard at our home. Our house is "U" shaped and surrounds a quiet courtyard. This year alone we hosted nesting pairs of eight different species. We sit out and enjoy it often in the summer, and one evening I listened to one bird call out, and then its mate answered. It made me think of a comment by Jens about "call and answer" musical patterns. It fascinated me in the moment, but I thought no more about it.

That night though, I woke up with that same melodic pattern repeating in my head. I went and picked up my guitar in the other room (it was 2:00 a.m.) to recreate and record the pattern with my iPhone. I went right back to sleep, and the next morning I had a new "pattern" to play with! I haven't put words to it or finished it, but I have it and I believe I will use it ... perhaps I'm just not ready yet. **Repeat a melodic pattern**, or *find* a melodic pattern. It can be a powerful first step to creation.

Just One Fret Apart

> **"The best and worst moments in life often lie close together. A beautiful note and an awful note are right next to each other, often just one fret apart."**
> — *Uwe*

The best and worst moments in life; I get it. I told you I play indoor soccer. I've played on average two nights a week for over fifteen years, and a few weeks ago I experienced this "best and worst" juxtaposition. On a Wednesday night, I scored a hat trick (a 3-goal game). It's not a great thing, but for me it's a significant and enjoyable achievement, a rarity even. Nine days later halfway through our Friday game, I hyper-extended my right knee. No contact, no foul. When I planted my foot to stop and turn, my leg buckled backwards. It took me six weeks to get back to playing. The best and worst. In May of 2012, I mentioned that I attended the first Kruger Brothers' Academy. I was supposed to go with my friend Davis. He plays banjo and first introduced me to the music of the Kruger Brothers. Unfortunately he wasn't well enough to make the trip with me. I called him each evening to tell him of the day's events and let him enjoy the experience vicariously. But one month later, Davis Holloway died of leukemia. The best and the worst.

Just one fret apart. Now what does it all mean to our music, specifically within the creative process? I believe this truth to be a lesson in patience or maturity, and also one of perspective. I mentioned earlier that as we grow and mature we get more comfortable with ambiguity. Ambiguity just means an inherent uncertainty, and the resultant lack of commitment. In these first few decades of the twenty-first century, we'd better learn to get comfortable with uncertainty. Musically and otherwise, ambiguity expresses itself as tension. And, guess what, tension is often *good* for the creative process! Purposeful tension, and then the release of it, makes for an exciting ride. Without tension, there is no joy of release; without anticipation there is no relaxation—and these two generally lie very close together. Only **one fret apart** sometimes. Lin-Manuel Miranda's phrase "wait for it" from the play "Hamilton" says it all for me. Wait for it … it's only one step away—and sometimes literally only one fret away. Have the patience and maturity to remember that with tension there is release very close at hand. Wait for it.

Now for perspective. **Just one fret apart.** I think this can also mean that when stuck, we don't have to start over from the beginning. We are perhaps, and probably already very close to magic. People like Uwe, Jens and Joel of the Kruger Brothers, they maintain perspective. I remember Jean Hatmaker of the Kontras Quartet rehearsing with me to perform a song I'd written and suggesting we stay on the "5" chord for one more measure. It seemed a miniscule change at the time, but it was just enough to build the tension that was missing at that point in the chorus. The trainer who I quoted in an earlier truth ("If you don't like it, it's because you need it") also preaches the simplicity of getting just "one percent better every day." Just one percent. **Just one fret apart.** It embodies patience and perspective in the creative process. Don't try to force a massive creative epiphany. Just wait for it; it's there. Creation is right there—perhaps only one fret away.

Don't You Stop It

> **"Creation doesn't always come easy. Sometimes our brains just have to run, like a computer—just don't you stop it by saying I can't."**
>
> — *Uwe*

This is one of my favorite lessons in music and life, and one I learned long ago. It's the perfect capstone truth for our study of the creation of original work. *"Just **don't you stop it** by saying I can't."* It comes down to the power of "core beliefs"—the foundation of how we view the world. Core beliefs form our take on—and what we expect of—the world, ourselves, other people, and the past, present and future. I've mentioned that I come from a Scottish/Irish heritage, but my core beliefs in fact run counter to some of the Scots' immigrant mentality that I grew up around. Two generations before mine, my grandmother and her sister worked as maids in mansions along Lake St. Clair in Grosse Pointe Shores. Traditional immigrant paradigms were to mind your station in life—and don't think about rising above it! But when my parents moved out of urban

Detroit in the 1960's they sought out anything they could afford in Grosse Point Woods. Granted, it wasn't along the lake (far from it), but it was within the five "Pointes" and we then attended Grosse Pointe public schools. The difference was, in that very different environment, young people believed they could do anything in their life. I then grew up with that core belief as well. I am not one to think or say, *"I can't."* On the contrary, I might even be described as just delusional enough to think I *can* no matter what. *"Just **don't you stop it** by saying I can't."*

Interpretation: presenting the music of others.

A Good Song ... It's Your Job ... Creation within You

> **"Don, there is a good song for almost anything you can imagine, and it's your job to find it. When you do find the right song for the right occasion, then you're doing your job. When you learn and perfect that song, that is creation within you!"**
>
> — *Uwe*

This conversation gave me an astounding *3 for 1!* I just can't in good conscience eliminate any of them either. *A good song for almost anything; it's your job to find it; and creation within you.* This is a great way to kick off our discussion of musical *interpretation* as opposed to composition ... of the creative process involved in presenting the music of others. Let's get at it.

A good song for almost anything. I'll start there. Depending upon whom you ask, the number of song *writers* throughout the last couple of thousand years of recorded history is thought to be over 15 million. The *current* song collection—those thought to exist right now—is estimated at 97 million songs (from the Gracenote database). If that isn't enough, the sum total number of songs ever to have existed is thought to top out between 2 and 5 *billion* songs. There probably already *is a good song for almost anything*. To some, this could be considered discouraging to the creative process. Some might believe there's nothing new to be written ... no creating left to do. But I got to thinking about the Krugers' discography on their website. Fifteen CDs are posted as of this writing, but only one in three consist of all original material. *Travel the Gravel*; *Up 18 North*; *Choices*; *Forever and a Day*; *Doc*; *Best Of*; *Christmas* and the *Scrap Books*—they're all beautifully, creatively arranged and masterfully presented—and they all contain songs not composed by the Kruger Brothers. I will add too, it's my experience that every Kruger Brothers show features the work of other artists, with "requests" for pieces they didn't write. Audiences love their *interpretation* of the piece, not their authorship. Johnny Cash or Willie Nelson wrote many moving songs; classics even. They also interpreted many more. There *is **a good song for almost anything**.* In fact, there are millions.

And it's up to me to perform that one in a million, at the right time and the right place. This truth, ***it's your job to find it,*** has opened my eyes—and lifted my musical practice. It has also made me conscious of things that in some cases I'd already been doing and wasn't aware of.

A friend and teammate asked me if I would "play" something at his son's high school graduation party. You know, thirty or forty people, young and old, enjoying the sunshine and celebrating this ritual of passage. *"Sure, I'd be happy to"* was my response. But later on I thought to myself, *"Wait, what am I going to do? What the heck should I play?"* ***It's your job to find it.*** I ended up doing two things. First, I'd collected all sorts of humorous life advice to the graduate from my other teammates (his father's teammates too). And I first recited those in performance (all I did with my guitar while discussing the advice to him was noodle with fiddle tunes as filler). Then when the jokes were done, I sang a song. The perfect song apparently. A song about a boy growing up; about the stages of his life; about what really matters in life. Well, the gathering loved it, but it was his grandmother that was *moved* by it. When I walked into the house for a coke a few minutes later, she followed me into the kitchen and hugged me. Weeping. Weeping, perhaps from joy and maybe a little bittersweet sadness too. I never expected the reaction, truth be told, I wasn't very happy with my performance. But her embrace and tears warmed me in a way few things can. I had *found* it. The right song for the right occasion. Unwittingly granted, but I had found it. I did my job.

*"Don, when you learn and perfect that song, that is a new **creation within you!**"* Interpretation as creation; it's *real*. Whether my humble efforts or the perhaps more lofty achievements of the brothers Kruger, creativity happens—even when you didn't write it! I've got more truths on the interpretive process, but these first few truths establish the paradigm. There is *a good song for almost anything; it's your job to find it,* to find a new **creation within you.**

I will never be the same again after holding a joyfully weeping grandmother. Just a fleeting moment, but a lifetime of impact (for me if no one else). That's interpretation as creation. It too is magic.

Set Your Intention

> *"I only write when I have to, Don ... when I find a topic that nobody's written a good song about, that's when I write—but otherwise I just find a good song, and then I become a time translator as any good singer should be. But it's really not about the notes you play; it is always about the intentions behind the notes. If we don't know our intention with a musical piece, no matter how perfectly we play, it doesn't mean a thing ... and once you set your intention, you don't have much choice anymore."*
>
> — *Uwe*

Set your intention. Intention could be defined as a "wish"; it could be construed as a "purpose" behind an act; or an aim that guides action. In any case, I think Uwe is simply asking that we consider the "why" of our play. He is asking that we premeditate our music—to play with purpose. And this might seem obvious, but in today's no-normal world, it's easy to become so distracted that when asked, we might be unable to identify purpose in anything we do. Don't get caught up; to create, let *intention* be your *first* consideration.

This truth resonates with me. Right up there with **discover what you see** and **put the play in playing music—set your intention** is in my top-five. If you understand it, if you internalize it, your musical practice will transform. It's that powerful.

Intention: *the thing that you plan to do or achieve ... what one intends to bring about ... your goal, purpose, aim, motive, hope, objective or design.*

Apply the whole definition to each and every song you set out to learn, otherwise, to use Uwe's term, you're just noodling. And the single word that embodies the definition? *Why.* Why will you learn, master and ultimately perform the chosen piece? More questions then blossom: why do I want to learn it? Who am I performing it for or singing it to? And what do I want to *evoke* with it?

I've discovered along this journey that the base intention of music *is* to evoke. The purpose of music is to evoke, to bring into the conscious mind of its performer or its audience, an *image*, an *emotion* or an *action*.

Want to know how to set your intention for each and every piece you add to your repertoire? Simply answer one question; *in learning this song, what do I want to see, feel or do—and upon hearing it, what do I want the listener to see, feel or do?* It's as simple as that. And may I add, if you can't answer that question—leave the song alone for now. Don't learn it until you *can* answer it. There is no right or wrong answer to the question, but when you have one, you have your intention.

Not Everyone Can Be Beethoven

"With someone else's music, we have a responsibility to another's lyric and melody. Not everyone can be Beethoven. Think about Blackbird; you can't do that better. Period. Ever."

— *Uwe*

After having this rolling around in my brain for several months now, I take away a few gems you might not expect. This whole movement on what it means to *create* in music was broken into *composition* and *interpretation*. We're dealing with the interpretive process now, and I think it's important to remember—this is someone else's composition. I didn't write the song, but just what *do* I owe the composer? Uwe spelled it out for me: I have a responsibility to a composer's lyrics and to the melody. I know I've seen performers change gender references or even add in a local adaptation intended to endear an audience. But I do know that such license to adapt is not one to be taken lightly. *To lyric and melody.* I respect and honor a composer's words and melody. But that leaves me free reign to harmony, rhythm and more!

The gem that has soaked in to my psyche here is Uwe's comment about Beethoven. He includes himself in this—**not everyone can be Beethoven.** I mentioned earlier my acceptance of the fact that I don't have enough time left on earth to play as well as Uwe, Jens and Joel, nor as well as countless other musicians. Along with that valuable self-knowledge comes the realization that I imagine I'll be doing much more interpretation than composition of music. That's OK, and what I imagine Uwe saying to me is, *"don't worry about being Beethoven— you just be Don."* I'll carry it one step further; his observation about "Blackbird" probably applies to many songs—and the lesson is, don't feel you always have to mess with it so much at all. Some songs are perfect just as they are. "For the Good Times" is perfect just as it is. "Blue Eyes Crying in the Rain" is already dead solid perfect. We have a lot of latitude for interpretation, but don't worry about trying to be Beethoven, McCartney, Nelson or Kristofferson ... you get the idea. You just be *you* recreating the work of McCartney, Nelson or Kristofferson.

The last lesson of value for me here is that there are in fact two sides to interpretation: first *learning* a song, and then *recreating* it. Learning and recreating, in that order. Now, let's look at a few more simple truths in light of this realization.

Just the Three Good Ones

> **"You don't need all 200 songs on a jukebox, Don, just the three good ones!"**
>
> — *Uwe*

Learn—***just the three good ones.*** Uwe said this to me very early on, soon after I met him actually. For me it's a lesson in focus. Now let's see if you're anything like me. Right this minute, today, while writing these words, I just stopped to take a quick inventory. I took stock of all of the songs I have somewhere in the learning process right now (*"Ouch"* he says as realization dawns). Would you believe I have ten songs that if asked I would have said I'm fairly seriously working on. There are also another twelve to fifteen songs where I've pulled the lyrics and "book-marked" a YouTube version with the idea of learning them.

And would you believe, I also have a book that I found while packing up and moving my mom's belongings. It sold for 75 cents back when she or her mother bought it in 1940. Mom used to play the violin. It's entitled "One Thousand Fiddle Tunes," and it is just that. It contains the names and music for the "A" and "B" parts of literally *1,000* fiddle tunes. I thought, *"Awesome, I can learn a new one every couple of weeks ... think of all the licks I'll learn!"* And, how far have I gotten with that? A man plans, and the gods laugh.

Just the three good ones. Check. You can imagine how well I'm doing at learning twenty or thirty new songs, plus a new fiddle tune every other week, oh and writing a book and make a living while I'm at it. To paraphrase Uwe earlier, perhaps some days I'm not playing a single note of real music. I told you earlier as well that I am actually a "rule of 3" kind of guy. I routinely apply that rule to so many important areas of my life— but apparently not to my musical practice.

That ends now. I just went to the current song list that I'd made as the inventory. I've highlighted three songs; one by the Kruger Brothers, one by James Taylor, and a third by Guy Clark. Those are the ones I'm going to learn right now. That's it; *just the three good ones*. I'm not saying the others I'd had plans for weren't good. It's sort of like when someone asks if you'd like a second or third cup of coffee and you hold your hand flat, palm down over your cup, and say "I'm good." It doesn't mean you'll never drink coffee again, or that you won't have a glass of wine this evening. It just means, you're good—for now. That's what I'm saying in selecting these three songs to learn. For now, I'm good. I'll focus right here on these three until I've truly learned them ... until I'm playing real music with them.

Cue the Movie

"You're not reading off of a script in your head while you're playing a song; it's more like a movie with pictures. It's important that you understand those images when you learn it ... then you can cue the movie the same way every time."

— *Uwe*

Learn—*cue the movie*. You know, I've been doing this. I didn't realize it at the time, but I've adopted it already. It began with the first simple truth I presented to you—*discover what you see*. This takes it to the next level. What we're seeing is really a whole movie, not just a single image, no matter how powerful it might be. It has setting, characters, time, action, dialog, and transitions. And *that* is what I have to learn first—the whole script, and the whole script as the composer saw it when he or she wrote it.

Let me give you an example. I said that I'm limiting my learning arena, for now, to just three songs. One of the three is "Carolina in My Mind" by James Taylor. Go look up the lyrics. The chorus is very warm and straightforward, and very easy for me to *cue it up the same*. Some of the verses however left me confused. I didn't know which images to cue up. In one verse, I was seeing heavenly images, but with an incongruous darkness. I was having trouble viewing the film because of this dissonance between heaven and darkness—until I started Googling the meaning of the lyrics. Then it clicked easily. Now I think I can cue the movie up reasonably close to James Taylor's vision. And that's the simple truth here. To learn a song, I have to first see the whole movie as close as I can to the songwriter's intention. Then I can start to learn it. That's interpretive learning. For most songs, if you look hard and long enough, you can find out what most lyrics meant to the songwriter (a possible exception that proves the rule might be Robert Hunter). That's interpretive learning. Later on we'll tackle interpretive re-creation. That still means to *cue the movie*—with your own intention. With your own personal movie reel.

———————

Before You Pick Up the Guitar

> *"Your goal is to back up the song. The song is the center. Listen to it a gazillion times before you pick up the guitar ... until you can sing it by heart—and with heart—until you know when you make a mistake with it."*
>
> — *Uwe*

Learn—*before you pick up the guitar.* It reminds me of Stephen Covey's classic book, *The 7 Habits of Highly Effective People*. If you've never read it, I highly recommend you do. His habit number three was to "put first things first." His message was to make sure you're making room for the important things in life to put first things first. But for us, it literally means to put first things first, to follow a proven sequence of events—to know the song *before you pick up the guitar.*

Not only have I broken the rule of three in my interpretive efforts, I also regularly do so by joyfully picking up my Martin and naively trying to jump right into a spectacular rendition. Of course, I'm reading the lyrics off of a sheet of paper. I'm referring to the chord designation and verse/chorus notes while I play it, and it's obvious even to me that I don't know the song. I always like the song, I might even *love* it. But, I don't *know* it. Uwe said, the song is the center; the first consideration. Without knowing the song, I am ill prepared to recreate it.

Before you pick up the guitar. My habit of finding and bookmarking a good version of the song on YouTube, or even several versions for that matter, is a good habit. I even do this first, as I should. My mistake lies in reaching for my guitar at that point. Instead, I need to wait, to have patience and learn the song ***before I pick up the guitar.*** It makes it easier really, and it sounds a lot better too. I can put in my ear buds and sing along to my heart's content. I can even cue up the songwriter's "movie" in my own mind while I'm learning it. And I can—and should—do all this ***before I pick up the guitar.*** Life is good.

———

Lyrics by Hand

> *"If you want to learn the song,*
> *write out the lyrics by hand.*
> *Printing them out from the Internet*
> *doesn't involve you at all."*
> — *Uwe*

Learn—*lyrics by hand.* He's right. I can print out "1000 Fiddle Tunes"—and be absolutely no further ahead than I was before I printed them out. **Lyrics by hand** means just that, with paper and pencil or pen, and not with a keyboard. This too makes a strong case for altered technology time and space. I believe I've mentioned that in my work "brain science" plays an important part. Professionally, I apply the latest developments in reference to what happens to our brains when we interact with others. But now we are talking about what happens to our brains when we literally pick up pencil and paper. It's not hard to look up.

When we write out *lyrics by hand*, we benefit in five key areas; calm, focus, creativity, retention and real estate. We now know that writing by hand has the same kinds of effects on our brain as meditation. The physiological side effects of slower breathing and heart rate mirror meditation's calming properties as well. Typing on a computer on the other hand, actually has the opposite effect.

We know that writing by hand versus computer means far fewer distractions and as a result tends to sharpen our focus. Through study with young students, we know that writing by hand increases creativity and the diversity of outcomes and process. Retention goes up steeply when we switch from keyboard to pencil. Simply put, our memory improves when we write it by hand over typing it out. And real estate? By that I mean we cover more ground. We involve more of our grey matter on both sides of the brain when we use a standard pencil.

Lyrics by hand. The standard graphite core wooden pencil was invented in the 1830's. Use it, pick one up and listen to the song over and over while you manually document the lyrics. Get *personally* involved in learning your next song.

Rhythm First

> *"Create the rhythm first ... then melody and harmony; that's the hierarchy of music. It's not critical that you hit all the right notes. It's always important that you hit the right rhythm."*
>
> — *Uwe*

Recreate—***Rhythm first.*** OK, I get it, there's a hierarchy to music. Who knew? And it really sounds profound, doesn't it? I felt a quite a bit of dissonance over this quote for while because I knew it was important. It was significant, but I wasn't sure why. Think about the terms and try to understand the traditional musical hierarchy of rhythm, melody, harmony. I couldn't. Why rhythm over melody, and melody over harmony? Finally, I set up a FaceTime call with Uwe to ask him about it (remember, he's a "visual"). I laid out my dilemma; the word hierarchy connotes a ranking ... often a ranking related to comparative power. Uwe, why does rhythm take priority over lyric? His answer made all the puzzle pieces come together in a very clear picture. *"Think of it as an order of development ... as if you are building a house."*

I get it now. You can dream about any room you want to: the master bedroom; the kitchen; a first floor laundry; a wrap-around porch. But the first thing you do is dig and build your foundation. It's a viable sequence, an "order of development." If the foundation isn't solid, the porch falls in. You don't build a room and then dig the foundation under it! By the same token, you begin with rhythm. Like a home's foundation, a song's rhythm underlies every element, every composition, every interpretation.

"Don, the rhythm is a baseline I can return to in case I get lost ... even when I learn a song, it is the rhythm of the words I learn first."

Just as some homes are built and even assembled in a factory and then delivered on-site, some music too seems manufactured and without any genuine foundation or intention. For my money, it's **rhythm first**.

Speak the Words

"As folk or blues singers, or whatever we want to call ourselves, we have to look at the words and how we say them. Speak the words. It cements the rhythm, the timing, the key."

— Uwe

Recreate—***Speak the words.*** I'll never forget my first Kruger Academy. I've mentioned that there were only five guitar players with Uwe. The hot seat was *HOT!* It wasn't the size of the audience you were in front of, it was the undivided attention you received from Uwe that warmed the seat. As I recall it now, I went first, or it could be I was just so nervous that it felt like it. I chose to play "Blackbird" for him. By nothing more than blind luck I had in fact set my intention with the song. I always see my three daughters and their growth and development when I sing it. I was proud of my interpretation of it in fact. When I finished, Uwe thought quietly for a moment and then suggested that I might speak the words in place of singing them. I was crushed. You might as well say I have the "perfect face for radio," or *"You want a second opinion? OK, you're ugly too!"* (Rodney Dangerfield). But, that wasn't Uwe's point. It was not a brutal qualitative assessment of my voice; it was positive, constructive counsel as to its beat, it's key and my phrasing—and the power of speaking the words along with the music— before singing them. At the beginning of this movement on creating music we considered the truth of **"first comes a picture"** and the power of visualization. The same holds true with the creative power of speaking out loud.

Speak the words. *"Don, the key and timing best for you come from how you would recite the words in speaking."* **Speak the words.** It follows his mantra of **"rhythm first"** (*vocal* rhythm), but years later he gave me the rest of the story. *"When you are learning, just strum the chords first and later see what you can fill in. If you want to learn a song, the words come first."* **Speak the words.**

––––––––––

Limit Your Scope

"When you learn and perfect a song, limit your scope. Work on four to eight bars at a time."
— *Uwe*

Recreate—***Limit your scope.*** Four to eight bars at a time. Most of us don't have the discipline. We try to immediately recreate a whole song's worth of the sound of many musicians with often many years of experience playing together. Start to finish. We foolishly assume we can absorb it, digest it and recreate it all at once.

Limit your scope. It reminds me of a very well known descriptive adage, "in the blink of an eye." Uwe once told us, *"Every time we blink, our brain resets. Try to work on just what you can play in between two blinks."* Give it a try. Just take on what you can play in the blink of an eye. Take just a few measures only—just four to eight bars at a time—and get that the way you want it *before* you move on. You'll find that's just about the right amount of "new" to take on with any given attempt at recreating the composition of another.

I think this is true of every part of life, professional and personal. Consider "kaisen"—the Japanese term for continuous improvement that grew across the automotive industry in the 1970s and 80s. It's been depicted as small, simple, positive acts that are continuously applied over time. Athletic trainers and coaches will tell you the same. One percent better every day to lose weight, get fit, and craft a healthy lifestyle. Why would music be any different? *Limit your scope* and succeed in ways you could never imagine possible!

Change It Up

"When I want to polish a song, the last thing I do is play games with it. Scales, tempo, anything to change it up—slow-fast, hard-soft, call and answer ... this contrast is often how I approach creativity."

— *Uwe*

Recreate—***Change it up.*** This is good advice in every part of our lives. In music, I've come to realize the overriding change-up is the interplay of tension and relaxation, dissonance and consonance. It's the reason why fiddle tunes have a Part-A and Part-B. It's why we strive to play up the neck, to apply note clusters at low, middle and high-end frequencies. Tension, release. ***Change it up.***

In my work with executives, managers, sales reps, service providers, and even parents with their children, *healthy* tension is not a contradiction in terms. Think about it: when tension gets too high, what happens? The 3-F's: freeze, fight or flight. That's not what we're after of course. But when tension gets too low, what do you get? Apathy. Healthy tension is what we're after. It's what makes life fun and exciting.

Change it up! You know, even healthy habits need a break. If you eat oatmeal and banana every day, your body adjusts. If you do the same exercise repeatedly, your body adapts. When you take the same route to work every day, your brain places the act into ritual. It will fill in the blanks while it works on something else. Your audience can and will do that too! *Change it up,* take a different way to work and see how it heightens your focus and awareness for the day. Then see what it does for your music!

Let It Rest

> *"I have this technique where I play something I'm working on very slowly. I may not get it right, but then I let it rest for a few days and don't think about it. The next time I pick up the guitar, all of a sudden it's there! That is a win for me."*
>
> — *Uwe*

Let it rest. Early within our discussion of one's life practice, Uwe impressed upon me the dynamic of our wanting success too fast. For me this is an important echo of that same concept. *Let it rest.* This isn't just observational, it's actionable. It is practical as well as theoretical. It is clear cut counsel to regularly and purposely set a creative work aside for a bit. To let something percolate, to let it rest, and to allow our subconscious to take over. My mom used to say, *"Patience is a virtue, possess it if you can ... found seldom in a woman, and never in a man."* Thanks mom! Old school but right on. And letting something rest, developing the *virtue* of patience, is even less common today.

We're not alone in this. There actually is such a thing as the "Pace of Life Project." Researchers involved secretly measured the speed at which pedestrians walk within city centers around the world. Asia and Western Europe clock in the fastest in covering a twenty-meter distance. The slowest appears to be the Middle East, with North America somewhere in between (except for New York City which came in seventh fastest around the globe).

The group in fact measured downtown walking speeds, as well as work speed (postal clerks) and even the accuracy of public clocks in thirty-one international capitals. Correlations? They show that a more hurried pace produces higher death rates from coronary heart disease, and higher rates of smoking and indigestion. I'm thinking our need for speed is also correlated with diminished creativity. Let me add insult to injury as well. We're getting worse. In the last twenty-five years, not surprisingly we've acquired ten percent more haste in our daily living—and nearly all of us even hurry along on moving escalators and sidewalks because they're just not fast *enough* for us!

My point? Learn to **let it rest.**

Rest: *a refreshing quiet or repose; mental or spiritual calm; an interval of inactivity; to be quiet or still.*

Give it a try. If nowhere else than in your creative musical efforts, give it a try right now. You haven't been to your journal in a while. Let's go there now. Hit the pause button. Do that. Consider each of the truths around creating in composition or interpretation. Which were especially meaningful for you? And why? Write them down now so you'll remember tomorrow and the day after. Sometimes it also helps to consider a higher calling in trying to create. Why do you want to write or learn new songs? For whom? Write that down too.

Here then is a final observation from Uwe to close out our study of the creative process.

> **"People think that the creative arts are about expressing ourselves, and it's not really ... it's about expressing our humanity. That's what good artists do."**
>
> — *Uwe*

Fourth Movement

PERFORM

Leave 'em Exhausted!

In the end, you have to perform something for somebody else. You can only really play when you step outside of yourself, out of your comfort zones, and play for another.

When it comes to Jens, Joel and I performing for you—we aint

young and we aint pretty, but we're as real as real can be!

To perform, you have to have a certain confidence, and you have to gain that confidence in front of every audience ... every time.

If freedom's just another word for nothing left to lose, then the first thing to lose is the fear of what other people think of you.

Songs are very personal. If somebody sings to you, there is nothing more personal.

That is all a listener really wants— confidence in you that you are going to finish this thing, that you know what you are doing … so hit just the first few notes, the first few words dead on and then it doesn't matter if you get shaky here or there, you already have them.

We don't have to do it all. If the mandolin is doing a chop on the offbeat, you no longer have to do it. On the guitar we think we have to do everything because the instrument has such range. It CAN do everything, but that's why we perform with others.

Our last movement—*perform*! The Kruger Brothers have been performing a long, long time—all around the world, since they were children. They *know* performance, and if you've been to one of their shows, you know that performing is when they are at their best.

Perform: *to carry out; execute; do … to fulfill or accomplish … as before an audience … to finish or complete.*

Our operational definition of the word perform—in a single syllable—is *do*. I can't put it any better than that. Any definition of performance also generally implies the *culmination* of methodical work or applied effort. *Perform.* It is the foundational intention of any music, to be performed, and Uwe is the ultimate performer.

––––––––––

Step Outside of Yourself

"In the end, you have to perform something for somebody else. You can only really play when you step outside of yourself, of your comfort zones, and play for another."
— *Uwe*

Step outside of yourself. I believe it's the end game of my musical practice, if not yours as well. Most of us *envision* at one time or another heroic scenarios of recognition, of ovation. We are seeing a completion of our practice, and the first step to make that vision a reality is releasing our inner voice to the *outside*.

Professionally I've been formed by the best when it comes to a behavioral approach. Paul Hersey used to say to me, "data has no power in a database, and it only affects others when you get the data out." That rings true for me in music—it only affects others when I get the music *out!* Uwe agrees, and adds another dimension.

Two Kinds of People

> *"Art for its own sake is valid, but it's not my way. There are two kinds of people—performing and non-performing. There is Jens and me; Jens is a scholar ... I am just a performer. I've never had that feeling for art for art's sake. The question is, do you perform for a God, or to please another person as I do. I would ask, how do you even know that the Gods are pleased?"*
> — *Uwe*

Jens is a scholar; perhaps a genius too really. He is an accomplished and highly creative composer. But can there not be two sides to Jens? Composer *and* performer. He is recognized as one of the most accomplished banjo players on the planet. He is so *because* he performs. **Two kinds of people.** It's a fun philosophical conundrum, but either way, Uwe is a performer at heart. I am as well. I play for people. My intention with a musical piece is targeted to its impact upon a listener. My intentions for this book are centered on the difference it can make in *your* life, not mine. In launching now into Uwe's wide world of performing, I'm reminded of his humble summary of a Kruger performance.

As Real as Real Can Be

"When it comes to Jens, Joel and I performing for you—we aint young and we aint pretty, but we're as real as real can be!"

— *Uwe*

When I coach managers or executives, I always begin by stating that my goal throughout any engagement is to *"help you be the best you that you can be."* It was Oscar Wilde who said over a century ago, *"Be yourself—everyone else is already taken."* Popeye always sang out, *"I yam what I yam and that's all what I yam!"* You just be you. **As real as real can be.** I'm counting on this last movement to help you one way or another to let that inner voice *out*.

My challenge with "*perform,*" as with the first three movements, was again sorting and organizing such a wealth of information. I ended up with *thirty* stand-alone simple truths about performing! However, my challenge turned out easier that I thought. Five very distinct groupings resolved themselves—each one clearly articulated by its own powerful truth:

1. Every audience, every time

2. The first thing to lose

3. Songs are very personal

4. All a listener really wants

5. We don't have to do it all

Join me now for a last wild ride!

Every Audience, Every Time

> **"To perform you have to have a certain confidence, and you have to gain that confidence in front of every audience, every time."**
> — *Uwe*

This truth, along with several more, establishes a foundational tenet of the art of performance. Some things have to happen with ***every audience, every time.*** When I speak to groups about the human side of enterprise, I may be working with wholesalers of Anheuser-Busch beverages, or medical equipment manufacturing personnel, Harley Davidson dealers, retailers with Bath & Body Works, bankers, fast food franchisees or engineers that design, build and operate power plants. Each and every one of them cries, *"but we are different!"* And in every instance they essentially are incorrect. People are people. The essentials of the applied behavioral sciences apply to ***every audience, every time***. And Uwe's right; *confidence matters*. Confidence impacts everything we *do*. He tells us we have to find that confidence with ***every audience, every time***. Let me net it out for you too: it comes only from *doing*. No pep talks, no encouragement from another will light it up. We have to *do* before confidence emerges. Success and confidence—they are forever inseparable. ***Every audience, every time.***

Make It a Personal Offering

"When you play and sing, make and hold eye contact with the person or group to whom you are playing. You are offering something—and with eye contact, you make it a personal offering."

—Uwe

Make it a personal offering—every time. Eye contact is a way to do that in any setting, including the one-on-many as when you're performing. Eye contact is best described as two people looking into each other's eyes—at the same time. *Locking* eyes is an apt description. Remember earlier when we talked about setting our intention when we're composing or interpreting a song? The point I'm reinforcing here is how our intention is generally to evoke—an image, an emotion, or an action in a listener. Eye contact is a powerful form of non-verbal communication, and it *will* evoke emotions and actions in others. It's an accelerant.

Granted, eye contact can be just like "Goldilocks and the Three Bears." As with the softness of the beds and the temperature of the porridge in the children's story, eye contact comes in three forms; too much (creepy), too little (scared, distracted or dishonest) and *"just right."* When it's just right, it can generate interest and trust from another. When used effectively, eye contact makes you more believable, even more likeable. And, guess what? Not only can it change another's perception of you, it can even change your own perception of yourself. Studies show that minimal intentional use of use of eye contact helps you to feel more confident and trust in yourself!

Make it a personal offering. It's the human side of performing. The functional or technical side of any endeavor has to be there. You have to have a song to sing, so to speak. But human competencies are real skills as well. When you ***make it a personal offering,*** you multiply the impact of your intention, your technique, your creativity and your mastery. Eye contact, facial expression, and body movement are all part of the *non*-verbal language at your disposal. Learn to speak that language to perform at your best!

———————

Catch It Right at the Start

"When you sing a song for somebody, take a second just to think about what the movie is like ... feed it properly into the projector (which is you) because when you catch it right at the start you will perform it with confidence."

— *Uwe*

Uwe's just talking about first impressions in your performances. I am in the people business, and I'm not new to the power of getting off on the right foot. We say "no second chance for a good first impression" for a reason. People draw conclusions about others very quickly—in fractions of a second. It happens on stage too! There are two questions we tend to ask—and then answer—about others within these first few milliseconds: do I *trust* this person (are they friend or foe) and do I *like* this person (am I attracted or repelled by them)? Very quickly we form a mental image of another individual—and in fact, with continued exposure to them, these first impressions will tend to become stronger, reinforced. We tend to validate them, and it's hard to change the impressions we've made in any significant way after that.

And the double-whammy? We are busy doing the same. During that same microsecond—we as a performer are assessing their reaction ... how we're coming across! We're conducting a real-time *self* assessment and it feeds into our confidence with the piece, and with the audience. What Uwe gives us here is a solid how-to in making sure our first impressions—and the first impressions of the songs we play—are positive. Remember, the audience and the performer are busy drawing conclusions around trustworthiness and attractiveness. When you want to **catch it right at the start**, threading the "movie" into our internal projector can greatly improve the odds of our hitting the first couple of bars dead solid perfect every time.

You Own the Stage

"If you take the stage to sing a song, you own the stage in that moment. Take advantage of it like a kid going to play in a sandbox. Don't worry about the mess you might make!"

— *Uwe*

Screw It Up All the Way!

"If you screw up, screw it up all the way. Those who are afraid to fail play timid and never experience that 'God, I AM alive' feeling."

— *Uwe*

This time we're taking on two at a time. **You own the stage** and **screw it up all the way.** Uwe's telling us not to worry about the mess we make in performing for others. He's also saying, if we do make a mess then we might as well make a *BIG* mess! I think what he's really talking about in both scenarios is *risk*—about what might be at stake in getting up on stage—and the best way to play the odds.

I've heard it said, *"in an unfair game, be bold."* The stakes involved in our getting up in front of people and performing are minimal. Stakes are simply the perceived cost or risk involved in any action, and unless you are a professional musician, the risks associated with performing reside just about exclusively in your head. Anticipation and anxiety over the mere possibility of catastrophe will often—no, *usually*—exaggerate the perceived cost of failure.

And what is Uwe saying? To be risk-*averse* means a strong tendency to always try to reduce uncertainty in an uncertain environment. On the other hand, risk-*seeking* behavior is just that, seeking out or embracing options that carry proven risk and significant stakes. But there is such a thing as risk-*neutral*, and that's Uwe's message for me. Samuel Clemmons once said, "I've seen a lot of pain in my life... and some of it even happened!" Uwe is saying go for broke; the stakes are negligible ... come on in, the water's fine! *You own the stage—screw it up all the way*, there's nothing to lose and *everything* to gain!

As an added note of comfort here, Uwe told me once: *"Don, a CD is not a performance— you expect it to be perfect. No one expects perfection on stage!"*

A CD is just a small, round polycarbonate wafer used to record, store and retrieve digital information. A CD can store and play back the digital *representation* of a musical performance. But, it is not a performance—it is an electronic recreation of one. It's another generation away from the performer. From a CD, from digital media and technology in general, we expect if not perfection, at least unfailing consistency in performance. Ever notice how upset we become when the cable box, CD player, Mega-Boom or especially our smart phones experience a glitch of some kind? Most likely *WAY* out of proportion to the inconvenience of the failure! We expect our electronics to work, first time, every time.

But, as performers, we're not made of polycarbonate plastic. As human beings we are not perfect, sometimes not even predictable ... and the audience *doesn't* expect perfection. I dare say the audience might even hope for the unexpected in a live performance. Thank you Uwe. What I hear you saying is—don't *worry* your life away, especially up on stage. Soak in the blessings instead.

It Shouldn't Cost You to Perform

"I once told a youngster 'never play for free kid,' and I mean it. Work should be compensated and it shouldn't cost you to perform."

— *Uwe*

It shouldn't cost you to perform. Well put Uwe, thank you. The question you raise is what is our work worth? As an author of five books in the last fifteen years, I believe I understand the creative process, and perhaps too the inherent pride in our creations. It takes time to create a work such as this. I only average a new one every three years. When it's done, you feel a powerful affection and sense of joy toward the creation itself. And then someone says, "Hey you wrote a book, can I have a copy ... would you give me one please?" That is verbatim by the way—*give* me one. Their expressed view of the value of my work is ... zero. **It shouldn't cost you to perform.**

There are times too in my speaking and coaching work when a prospective client will call me to discuss a possible engagement. We get along great and it's obvious that there's a match between their needs and my experience. They ask if we can meet at their offices in New York to take the discussion to the next level. This is when I enthusiastically agree to meet with them at no charge (remember, this isn't the engagement yet) provided they cover my travel expense. Even airfare and ground expense to the city alone can run a grand or more. Most individuals agree to the tradeoff without hesitation. But there are some that push back saying, "You want me to pay your expenses to come sell to me?" What they want is my expertise to help them craft their intervention with their people, and they are telling me they value my contribution at exactly *zero*. Matter of fact, they believe my involvement is worth so little that I should be excited to "buy" the opportunity at only $1,000. I don't judge. It is their decision to make. I just don't make the trip. Equity theory is all about the perceived balance between contribution and reward. If we check this sense of equity—it's within all of us—chances are we won't say "yes" when it just isn't right. ***It shouldn't cost you to perform.***

I'd like to tell one last story on this. I know a highly respected speaker and coach. He receives millions every year for what he does—even when he does it for *free!* Yep. He does *pro bono* work for the likes of the Girl Scouts all the way up to our nation's military academies, and all manner in between. Now, here's the catch; the organization receiving his "free" services cuts him a check up front for the full market rate of those services (it's a *lot!*). He never cashes the check, and when he's done with the engagement he signs the check back over to the organization. He does this to generate commitment, ownership and investment on their part. In doing so, their valuation of his services becomes full market rate! ***It shouldn't cost you to perform.***

Karma is Pay

> *"Performing at a senior center is paid. Your pay is just different. Karma is pay. Money isn't the only way you can get paid."*
> — *Uwe*

Now for "***karma is pay.***" I'm actually performing at a senior center this week. I do so most weeks lately. I receive not a penny, but the pay is handsome! And a double bonus? My mom lives there. She suffers from Alzheimer's and is most often unaware she's even had a visit from me—until I started bringing the guitar. ***Karma is pay.*** Now, if I don't bring it, the first thing she'll say is, "you didn't bring the guitar this time"? ***Karma is pay***. When I play for her, the day room with eight or ten of her peers present takes on a beautiful new mood—a mood that has nothing to do with the meds they're all on. ***Karma is pay***. "Free" doesn't mean unpaid. In fact, I've said several times that the guiding focus behind my professional effort now is helping people with people. My dharma, my goal in life now though, is to give gifts that cannot be repaid. Anywhere I can, anytime I'm able. And, the *only* pay I seek? *Karma*. Without a doubt the richest I have ever felt in my life was the result of my having given such a gift. A single gift. A few years ago, when I subbed out to recover on the bench of a soccer match, I asked my teammate standing next to me (between gasps for air) how he was. I expected "not bad" or "fine." Instead, he looked off into the distance and said, "Not well." I said I was sorry and asked him what was up. He's from the UK and he explained that his sister was very ill and she was going to die. He explained he didn't have the money to fly over to say goodbye and that he was very sad.

When I got home, I checked my airline miles. Not enough. I called American Express to see how many points I had there that could be converted to miles. Still not enough. The American Express rep pointed out that if I wanted to convert my "Gold" card to "Platinum" (the fees are higher) there would be a 50,000-point bonus for my account. Enough points! I called my teammate for his mileage account number. I moved AmEx points into airline miles. I moved the airline miles from my account to his and booked his flight. He made it to England in time to spend the last four hours of his sister's life with her and said goodbye. ***Karma is pay.*** Never before had I felt so rich. I wanted nothing in return, and ever since that day I have looked for opportunities to give such "gifts that cannot be repaid." But perhaps it *is* repaid—in karma.

I tell you this not with any sense of "paying it forward" either. That concept is one of giving, along with a call to pay it forward to another in need rather than paying it back. Some even admonish that when you receive such a gift, you have to pay it forward three-fold. I'm not built like that. I'll quote a friend, "If you want a better world, *you* just go first." That's all I'm trying to do, to go first.

And guess what? I am never as wealthy or as happy as when I can uncover the chance to give these gifts. Let me ask a favor too— *tell* others about the good turns you take in life. I'm not advocating bragging, simply spreading evidence of good news in a sea of tension and conflict in our lives these days. Give a gift that can't be repaid. Big gifts or little gifts—they all pay massive dividends. **Karma is pay.** Karma rocks.

The Microphone is Always On

> **"When you decide to perform, then take the mindset that you are always performing ... the microphone is always on. In fact, that's when I play my best. You're never playing for yourself—it's always for another ... a fly on the wall, an empty chair."**
>
> — *Uwe*

The microphone is always on. You are always performing. All day, every day. The mic is on. Why? Because it's a behavioral world. We impact others through our behavior—and the people we impact are professional *watchers*. I tell leaders all the time, the people who report to you are professional *boss* watchers. Sometimes the slightest suggestion from the boss becomes an order to the receiver's ears. Your children are also adept at parent watching (scary). If you cuss or smoke, your children to some degree will cuss or smoke—regardless of what you tell them to do or not do. *The microphone is always on.* In performing, we are always under a microscope, always creating impressions—positive and negative. The question is, are we aware and purposeful in our performances, at home or on stage? Wherever you are, plan on a live mic and a live audience. *The microphone is always on.* Every audience, every time.

Five Tunes Ready

"You have to have five tunes ready no matter how drunk or tired you are."

— *Uwe*

Five tunes ready. It's funny, but Uwe never used to focus so strongly around the art of performance in his lessons with me as he has the last year or two. Perhaps I wasn't ready for it yet. Either way, these golden truths are real! *Five tunes ready.* I get it, as a performer you always need to have five tunes at the ready ... ya just never know. But I'd like to add some interpretation too. For me, what Uwe is referring to here is "jamming". Jamming in a group, often a large group and often strangers. What I'd like to add is that I need to have five tunes at the ready at any given time—and I prefer them to be *simple* and/or *familiar*. My experience with jams is that most often people are trying to show how good *they* are. They want to win. They want to shine and shine alone. I've learned that I have the most fun when I play songs that are either simple enough for everyone to pick up and join in very quickly, and/or familiar enough that they already know the song (in their heads if not in their hands). **Five tunes ready.** What are your five tunes? If you sat down tonight with six or eight strangers to jam for a bit, what would you play when it's your turn? Write those titles under *five tunes ready* in your journal, and then come on back.

Know What You Sound Like

> **"Prepare and rehearse with the same electronics you'll use to perform. Know what you sound like."**
>
> — *Uwe*

As I've said on a few other occasions—this must to be obvious to everyone but me— **know what you sound like.** Much as we might record a performance to critique or send out for feedback, you want to hear yourself as an audience would. You want to know how far you should be from the mic, what microphone to use or how many. Uwe was kind enough to give us some basic performance pointers:

- Always use the same pickup (e.g. Fishman Gold)

- "BYOA"—bring your own amp, pre-amp and microphone—those are what create your sound

- Try these—the "RedEye" pre-amp, with a "Zoom A3" for effects, and a "Spacestation" V.3 Stereo Monitor

Whether you choose these or others, use the same equipment each time, every time—rehearsing or performing. **Know what you sound like** while you're playing, not after. Added bonus? To get the best sound, think about *positioning* of electronics too:

- Sing *over* the microphone, don't block your face with it

- Put a guitar mic (if you don't have a pickup) *below* and to the left of the sound hole

- Experiment with just the right spot for placement of a single-mic performance.

Know what you sound like. In fact, I've realized that the use of electronics such as these are part and parcel of getting to a certain point along a path as a practicing musician. I think I'm getting close now.

Leave 'em Exhausted

"Playing music is communicating, you share your vision. You can talk about it just so long, and when you perform it—leave 'em exhausted!"

— *Uwe*

Uwe's final notes on what needs to happen with *every audience, every time*, are all about your end game and the irresistible power of self-disclosure or the giving of oneself. Sharing a vision is from the heart and has to be felt. It's not enough to just be understood, seen or heard—it has to be *felt*. Share your vision. Simply noodling and revealing nothing of your point of view about life, death and everything in between isn't Uwe's way. I asked about his ultimate strategy in performing, specifically whether he purposely held back to leave an audience wanting more. His eyes twinkled and he smiled; *"No Don, **leave 'em exhausted!"*** Exhausted. *Every audience, every time.* Share your vision and ***leave 'em exhausted***. If you do, they will be back!

The First Thing to Lose

"If freedom's just another word for nothing left to lose, then the first thing to lose is the fear of what other people think of you."

— Uwe

What got you here won't get you there ... I've mentioned it before. We're all in the business of doing something *different*. And this isn't something to start doing, this is something to stop doing ... just a few separate truths about giving something up, about **the first thing to lose** when it comes time to perform. *Fear.*

Uwe once said to me, *"Everyone can noodle, but to sing a song with heart, nicely—that is being naked in front of a thousand people— it's a beautiful, scary thing."* Beautiful and scary. That is the paradox, the vision attracts and the reality frightens. *"**The first thing to lose** is the fear of what other people think of you."* Easier said than done, right? The reason it's so tough to conquer is that fear and excitement are physiologically the same. Same brain signals, and the same chemicals that energize our body for fight or flight. Remember, we've been *programmed* for fear in many cases. As a matter of fact, our default when we're not sure *is* fear. Let's just focus on what to do about it:

1. Use it and acknowledge it; don't deny it

2. Perhaps I can't turn the fear into out and out excitement, but maybe I can dial it back to healthy anticipation

3. The power of self-affirmation is undeniable; talk to yourself—in a good way—even if you don't believe you yet.

4. Engage audience members, *talk* to people beforehand and it becomes a conversation, not just a performance. Direct your attention to voices *outside* of your head—*their* voices.

Uwe always says it takes fifty times to get a song right, to ritualize it and put it in the automatic centers of our brains. Perform a piece literally 50 times and the fear will evaporate for most of us too. I've coined the term *"the law of 49"* for a bonus simple truth if you will. Most of us want to skip the first forty-nine performance and get right to the 50th and knock 'em dead like Uwe, Jens and Joel. Life don't work that way. Follow the law of 49—put in that time—and there will be no more fear.

I'll add another physical cue here: *burn* it off! Move around; go out and chat with your audience to literally burn up some of the chemicals of fear! I know that Tony Robbins, the motivational speaker, spends time on a small jogging trampoline backstage before a performance. The cool part is you can use this movement to either get rid of adrenaline or to build some up when you're feeling low. Finally, just let added time get rid of fear. I believe that at age forty you officially don't have to care, at fifty you really don't, and at sixty ... what were we talking about? Ah yes, the fear of what others think of us. Let it go.

Get Your Teeth Apart

"When your jaw is locked, it is a sign of being either scared or aggressive. It's normal. When you start to sing to someone your adrenaline takes over ... but the sexy part about being a singer is to overcome it and sing a brutal truth without panic.

Your can manage with an audience of 5,000 people below you by not giving in to instinct ... and the easiest way to do that is to get your teeth apart, to relax your jaw and tongue. We often have a fear of letting out our thoughts. That causes you to clench, and that creates uncertainty in the listener ... he doesn't know if he can trust you or not."

— *Uwe*

What a beautifully simple cue to chill out; **get your teeth apart.** Teeth clenching (psychologists call it "false chewing") is indeed correlated with fear, anger, and anxiety. It is a non-verbal cue within interpersonal communication that signals internal struggle. No wonder an audience might wonder about us when they see it. Just **get your teeth apart**—simple as that. I've tried it and it works. If clenching is a result of anxiety, then consider working it in reverse. *Un*-clench to release the anxiety. It reminds me of another powerful physical cue we use to teach people to ride horseback; "heels down" is what a riding instructor will command a student—and the rider is transformed. Uwe's simple command to **get your teeth apart** can transform a singer, transform a song and literally release fear from the body.

Uwe and I had a long discussion about other things to watch out for, about what else gets in our way. Our discussion resolved into a triad of performance traps, the first being this *fear*. Fear probably is the strongest and most predictable of the traps we will all face in our quest to progress and perform. But what happens when we conquer fear, then what embodies the next performance trap? In a word, *certainty*. When we no longer fear, I believe we run the risk of believing we always have the answer. The risk becomes one of closing ourselves not just to the fear, but also to other truths, cues and perspectives. There's nothing worse than an arrogant performer.

And the final challenge to effective performance, the last of the performance traps? Perhaps we can call it *fatigue*. I've spoken to several experienced and successful performers who tire of the road, the grind, the business, even their band mates and the audience itself. Some want to devote more time to composing, some to their families. Maybe it's just a natural tiring of the "same old-same old." Wherever we are on the path, we're always looking for something new and shiny, and the cycle begins anew. Performance traps are real, but when anticipated and combated effectively they can be overcome. I've progressed far enough to experience all three over the course of my life's practice. With my musical practice, I'm still working on the first two! Fear, certainty and fatigue … **get your teeth apart** to cure the first.

———————

Songs are Very Personal

"Songs are very personal—if somebody sings to you, there is nothing more personal."

— *Uwe*

I think some of us forget just how intimate a song is meant to be. They *are* personal, for both parties present—performer and listener. Throughout the book, we've crafted in detail the very "personal" nature of a musician's practice: the child within; the pursuit of happiness; what our parents played; who matters to us and just the right path for each of us—it's *all* personal. But what about the listener's path? Theirs too is a very personal journey. Think about what goes through the mind and heart of your listener when you perform for them.

We have talked about setting our intention with a piece ... about what we want to evoke in a listener. Emotions, thoughts, actions. These are very personal to each and every person seated in front of you. Will your song recall thoughts of their days past? Will it awaken a long-forgotten feeling of love or loss, or a profound, enjoyable excitement in the moment? The result is personal for both of you.

Personal: *coming from or intended to a particular person and no one else; related to* *private aspects of a person's life; intimate, secret.*

Performance is really quite a special relationship—and sometimes we forget that. Outside of music, leadership is very personal, as is parenting, coaching, selling, serving—all interactions of an intensely *personal* nature. It's easy to let that slip in a no-normal world. My intention, as I write these words, these songs of simple truth, is very personal to you and I as well.

Love a Song Before You Learn It

"Make sure you really love a song before you learn it—you may be playing it for a long time."
— *Uwe*

How about—just make *sure* it's personal. Think about what you put into a song! Like listening to it "a gazillion times," scribing the lyrics by hand, creating your own interpretation and presentation of the piece, perhaps arranging for others. And then let's not forget—performing it *fifty* times to ritualize it and get it just right. That is a significant investment. Of time. Of energy. I often use the phrase, "hire tough, lead easy" with my coaching clients. When you take someone on to work for you, it is a massive expenditure literally and figuratively. Get the *selection* right and life is good. Get it wrong and not so much. The same is true of every song you choose. **Love a song before you learn it.**

When a Song's Over, It's Over

> **"Each song has a timeline too. If you linger over a song, you take time from the next one. When a song's over, it's over."**
> — *Uwe*

When I sing and when I teach, there are certain anecdotes, set-ups and punch lines that I know will work with every audience every time. I use them every audience every time, same time and same place. Often family related, customer centered or just plain fun and funny. I use them always. And other times ... I just make my point. I just tell the story. I just sing the song. When I first began public speaking for a living, it generally took the shape of an eight-hour day in the classroom. That might seem a daunting task to keep eight hours of content presentation, facilitation and application activities straight in my head, but it's not. There is a timeline for every part of it. It is just a series of twenty-minute segments or experiences, each with its own timeline. There is a "set list" for it.

Every *musical* performance has a set list, and each song has a concrete timeline. Whether you set it up with humor or emotion, or whether you just tell the story—every one has a distinct timeline. If we dwell too long on one, we throw off the next. And the next. So, **when a song's over, it's over.** We discussed a relevant truth earlier on in our movement on one's musical "practice"—that **everything ends.** Well, every song will end too. Every song *needs* to end. **When a song's over, it's over.**

All a Listener Really Wants

> **"That is all a listener really wants; confidence in you that you are going to finish this thing, that you know what you are doing."**
>
> — *Uwe*

Confidence in me; it's **all a listener really wants.** That's it. He just hopes I know what the heck I'm doing. She wants to know I'm going to see it through properly.

All a listener really wants. In fact, it's all anyone really wants from any interaction. My old boss used to say, *"leadership is influence."* Period. Whether in an organizational setting, singing onstage or at home with your children—any performance is influence—

and vice versa. And with some jobs, such as being a parent, the need to lead goes on a long time. Performing is a need-to-lead role. What did Uwe say? *"When you take the stage, you own the stage?"* My read there is that when you take the stage, you take the lead.

All a listener really wants is confidence in you leading them. This influence parallel between leading and performing also brings to mind something I read recently about the millennial generation and their expectations of a boss. The article's point of view was that younger people want a "coach" and not a manager ... that they have been coached most of their lives by someone who isn't family (all sports today are *organized* sports). They want someone to keep developing their path, cheering their progress and to be there. Sound familiar? Perhaps millennials, like listeners, just want to have confidence in the hands in which they've placed their career. My youngest daughter works for a software firm of 10,000 employees, with an average age of twenty-eight. I'm thinking most of those 10,000 just want a boss they can have confidence in; confidence that she knows what she's doing, and that she'll see it through. That's all our listener really wants from us—confidence in the hands in which they've placed themselves for the evening.

You Can Only Lose It

"An audience will give you their trust quite easily. They will trust their feelings for you, and you can only lose it from there. We're always taught that we have to earn respect. No. They will give it readily, but then we earn the right to keep it!"

— *Uwe*

Trust, like empathy, is organic. Through exhaustive study, we know a *lot* about empathy and the human connection. Trust falls under the same umbrella, and some of the same simple truths. **You can only lose it.** We are born to connect, to trust, to understand and care about others. Through empathy we connect very easily. We're wired to do so. In a full hospital nursery, when one newborn cries they all cry. When we meet others later in life we, in most cases, still trust and connect easily. And we also still take it back if our trust is proven unfounded. **You can only lose it.** A profound simple truth in music and in life. Have you ever been introduced for a performance and receive that welcoming applause? You haven't done anything yet, but you receive an ovation. That's trust, gladly and easily given, and **you can only lose it.**

There are No Thrones

> **"There are no thrones in music ...
> the player and listener are one.
> There needs to come a point when
> you step outside yourself and see
> your presentation ... you become a
> part of them."**
>
> — *Uwe*

No thrones—two syllables and so much power. Uwe says we "arrange" for the audience too. I draw a couple more conclusions here. The first has to do with self-knowledge. The hallmark of any highly effective performer in any arena is knowledge of self. It's how we gage and manage our impact on others. The only route to knowing oneself is to put ourselves in the eyes and shoes of the other. *"There comes a point where you step outside yourself."* It's like court sense or field sense in athletics—ya gotta get your head up.

There are no thrones. There are two forms of power in leadership, of influence potential: *position* power and *personal* power. Position power is given to you by an organization—the standard rewards and punishments basically. But personal power is given to you by your people, your followers ... and then maintained by earning it back. Sound familiar? **There are no thrones.** Within musical performance there are no trappings of position power. ***There are no thrones.*** With personal power, you can't *make* a listener like you; you can't force them to enjoy what you offer. They'll give you the stage, but you earn the "second" ovation. ***There are no thrones.***

Performing Carries Responsibility

> *"You never know what you will evoke in a listener when you perform. Be careful—performing carries responsibility."*
>
> — *Uwe*

I offer one last cautionary truth around our discussion of the listener in the performance equation. ***Performing carries responsibility.*** Think back to the prelude to this book. I told you about my epiphany surrounding Uwe's advice to discover what I *see* when I play a song, of how when I now perform Tim O'Brien's "Late in the Day," I see my mom alone trying to recreate a life-long ritual at the close of the day. ***Performing carries responsibility.*** Now for the rest of the story. I performed that song for an academy audience the following year, with that very same setup and discussion of my mother's struggle late in life. I mentioned the shining eyes and warm hugs of so many in response to the song that weekend. There was one reaction I didn't mention. One man came to me later with a heartfelt embrace and tears in his eyes. He told me, *"Don, to make a long story short I've had a terminal diagnosis. I don't have long for this earth and I wanted to tell you how deeply your performance moved me. Thank you. You see, what scares me most about leaving this world is how I'll soon be leaving my wife alone late in the day. I wish she could have heard your performance with me, Don."* Wow, be *careful* what you evoke in others—***performing carries responsibility.***"

We Don't Have to Do It All

> **"We don't have to do it all. If the mandolin is doing a chop on the offbeat, you no longer have to do it. On the guitar we think we have to do everything because the instrument has such range. It CAN do everything, but that's why we perform with others."**
>
> — *Uwe*

I can count on both hands the number of times I've performed on stage with other musicians. It's uncharted waters for me. I haven't got my fifty reps in yet. But I love it. I talked earlier about the frustrations I've felt in trying to recreate songs on my own, of trying to replicate the energy of a piece not only performed by experienced professionals—but by a bunch of them! But like Uwe says, *we don't have to do it all.* That's one reason we want to perform with others—that and the richness of the experience and the music.

I've had the honor one time of playing and singing with people that perform for a living, including a world-class cellist. In the process, I discovered that again, truth is truth regardless of the setting. In my coaching practice, one of the toughest challenges an executive can face is letting go. As their followers grow and develop, what they need and want from their leader is *autonomy*. Letting go of our ego needs and empowering others is a very difficult thing in leadership, yet I found the musical equivalent exhilarating! *We don't have to do it all.* Arranging my own song to include others' instrumental tones and vocals allowed me to easily step outside of myself, and improved the end product tenfold! *We don't have to do it all.* Take a deep breath and let go. The most effective people at any challenge are always those who surround themselves with people that can outperform them! Embrace it.

We don't have to do it all. Uwe says that's what the *banjo* is for. For me this delightful truth is best understood with a favorite movie quote. I mentioned earlier that I grew up soaking in a male worldview from the Duke and Clint Eastwood. What applies perfectly here is from Clint Eastwood's "Magnum Force," the second movie in the "Dirty Harry" series. After dispatching the last bad guy to end the film, Clint says to the corpse, *"A man's gotta know his limitations."* Ditto, the guitar player. After all, that's what the banjo is for.

Create Space

> **"Bluegrass music is so intriguing because it sounds so fast. Everybody in the band is playing very simple elements, alone not doing much, but together they sound like a million dollars. Leave space, create space where you don't play."**
>
> — *Uwe*

Create space. In playing soccer, creating space, moving to space and finding space is a never-ending mantra. It's a never-ending quest. Now add the rest of the story to this simple truth—"***create space*** *where you don't play."* Now we're talking. Just like a give-and-go in the world's game, musically we want to allow for, and even create, the opportunity for others to play (where *we* don't). A musical give-and-go. In organizational performance, we have identified a very destructive habit on the part of leaders—winning too much. When it's important; when it's meaningless. Some people always want to win. Some always want every space and everything that goes with it. I imagine in musical performance, a failure to uncover space, and then respect it and allow for its use by others would be just as short sighted, just as alienating. *Create space* where *you* don't play. Rest. You'll be amazed at how good it sounds!

Uwe added a cultural twist that might illuminate some of our tendencies too:

> *"To have something do the work for you, and pretend you are very busy is very American. In Germany we do the opposite; we try to encompass a lot, but make it look like nothing (it makes us look very smart). This is bluegrass. You do as little as possible to accomplish your goals."*
>
> — *Uwe*

Nice. *Create space.*

———————

If You are the Vocalist, You are Leading

> *"In music, yes there is always a master drummer setting the rhythm, but understand—if you are the vocalist, you are leading. Most people don't have the ability or experience to discern all the elements of music, to take sound apart into its separate elements— but if you are going to lead, then you have to hear it all."*
>
> — *Uwe*

Now he's talking my language. ***If you are the vocalist, you are leading.*** An important part of my own study is figuring out who is going to lead as a foundational diagnostic tool. Think about it; if one of your people is performing to standard—who should lead? *They* should! With their performance, they have earned self-direction. If they are not able to perform adequately, you need to lead or the work won't get done. It's very simple.

This truth is even more simple. ***If you are the vocalist, you are leading.*** It removes any confusion. *You* need to lead. This works for me because I love to sing. I also love to lead. If someone else is going to sing, they need to lead. In performing with others instrumental only, then in my book, the one who owns it leads it. What I mean is, let the one who brings the song lead it. Whoever has the intention or provides the vision behind the piece should be the one to lead it—but leading too carries responsibility. If you're going to lead it, you'd better hear it all. The bass player, the cellist, the banjo, mandolin and fiddle. Still want to sing it? *If you are the vocalist, you are leading,* and leading, on stage or off, carries responsibility.

A Chord in Unison

"To play the exact same notes as someone is almost impossible, the slightest variation will give you away—but if you play in harmony it will just sound like a chord in unison."

— *Uwe*

A chord in unison. A chord is just three or more musical notes in unison. In harmony. It explains a lot, and it integrates nicely (in harmony) with other truths. *Do less, not more ... Create space.* This string of truths fell right in my lap during a performance I put on recently with a banjo player. I found that by just playing on one or two strings, behind and in simple harmony with the banjo, it sounded wonderful! It can be several musicians in harmony, and for the listener—*a chord in unison*.

Take Care of the Other

> *"Take care of the 'other.' Whether it's banjo, mandolin, piano, fiddle, bass—take care of them. It takes your attention away from yourself and takes your ego out of the game ... it directs your attention outside of you and puts compassion first."*
>
> — *Uwe*

Empathy over ego. Listen more, talk less. Seek first to understand, then to be understood. *Take care of the "other"*—in music and in life. While I strongly advocate taking care of oneself as a *first* step to caring for others (put your own mask on first), it's then incumbent upon me to take care of the other. Notice how these final performing truths are building to crescendo one upon the other? I believe that's because performing is a pinnacle reached via the truths surrounding our play, our practice and what it takes to create. Performing isn't for everyone, but you wouldn't be reading this if it wasn't meant for you. Take the lead, but "*take care of the 'other'*"—it's what we do.

Arrange for the Audience

"When you arrange music, you arrange for the audience too. They are part of the arrangement, part of the other."

— Uwe

Last year I accompanied Uwe to the Kruger Brothers gig at the *Isis Restaurant and Music Hall* in Asheville, NC. It allowed us a couple of hours in the car together to get there, time in between (they played both Friday and Saturday nights) and more targeted conversation on the way back to Wilkesboro on Sunday. The time together was awesome and we got a *lot* done that weekend. But I hadn't bargained for the simple truth that came up in the green room before their performances. **Arrange for the audience too.** They determine the evening's set in "green room time" before a performance. Always. They've meticulously arranged their play and interplay in rehearsal back in the studio. They often appear to be improvising wildly during a performance. But don't let your joy in listening fool you, the improvisation is rehearsed (if I can say that). What is determined on the spot is the *evening's* arrangement. The night's performance is arranged on site. Asheville is different from Ann Arbor, and from Ontario too. Your first-born is very distinct from the baby of the brood. Each audience too is very distinct, and *is* part of the other. When you and yours get ready to perform, don't forget to **arrange for the audience.**

Better Every Round

> **"Rehearsing means following a premeditated course to get better every round. Rehearsing is committed effort. Rehearsal is anticipating a certain situation and planning for execution, when someone gets married you have a rehearsal dinner—because you want to get used to it."**
>
> — *Uwe*

One final truth of performance and taking care of the other. Rehearsal. When the Kruger Brothers rehearse, it is all about trying to *get **better every round***. That's why their performances can be so breathtaking— they've fought a lot of rounds together! I can only imagine the amount of rehearsal that has gone into their work. Perhaps the evolutionary sequence of a performance is just that; *create* or learn it, then *rehearse* to get used to it, and then *perfect* via successive iterations. Uwe calls that pinnacle "remembering together."

SING

They Just Might Ask!

When you walk through an airport carrying a guitar, no one will ask you to play ... but they might ask you to sing. Learn to sing!

Every word you sing is like a conversation. Don't swallow the words. Make sure you are understood. Be precise, as if you're giving instructions to a five-year-old.

Don, you have to sing the song as beautifully as possible ... then you will be the king of every jam session.

We've been lied to so many times we don't trust anyone anymore, but when you sing, we can tell a lie immediately. You cannot concentrate on lying and singing at the same time ... so when you want to say something with your music—mean it.

The Lord likes you when you work—but he loves you when you sing!

The word "CODA" refers to the concluding passage of a movement or composition. The concluding passage of this work, this coda, is entitled *SING!* Uwe is an excellent storyteller—a powerful man of voice, providing *all* of the primary vocals for the Kruger Brothers. What I find fascinating here is, again, the inherent crescendo within this work.

Play ... Practice ... Create ... Perform—all rising, all building one upon the other. And now, in peaceful signature—*Sing*. Some 40,000 words ago, I asked you to consider each movement a personal, enthusiastic exhortation from Uwe himself. This concluding passage is no less meaningful for its calm. To quote a friend, *"The Lord likes you when you work—but he loves you when you sing!"* Only three short simple truths remain here in closing, but each one provides a certain integration of the dozens we've already absorbed.

Sing: to produce melodious sounds; to tell a story in song or verse; to chant, croon, serenade.

Learn to Sing!

"When you walk through an airport carrying a guitar, no one will ask you to play ... but they might ask you to sing. Learn to sing!"

— Uwe

Telling a story in song or verse—it's been going on for thousands of years. To entertain, to educate, even to maintain popular cultural practices and beliefs. Some folks can't carry a tune in a bucket; others can cover or mimic any style or performer you give them. Some of us just plain sing.

Our singing voice is a byproduct of our physiology and of our likes and dislikes. To use an earlier organizer, our voice too is often a product of "what has stuck" over the years. For me, in no particular order, the voices that stuck were Ray Charles, Ray Price, Lennon *and* McCartney both, Tony Bennett, Merle, Elvis, Hank, B.B. and Smokey just to name a few. How about you, whose voices would you love to have? Bonnie Rait or Emmy Lou? Allison Krause or Aretha or Patsy? It too is personal.

*"They might ask you to sing. **Learn to sing!**"* The operative term here is "learn." It's not just the expression of raw emotion that makes a singer (except for Janis). There is technique involved, and it can be learned. There's even

such a thing as "vocal pedagogy," the study of vocal instruction. I've isolated three must-haves for an effective voice:

1. Breath—your lungs are the bellows; they gotta be fit for it

2. Posture—if the physiology is wrong, it either won't work, or it takes too much work

3. Training—like any other pursuit of competency, the right teacher will multiply your talent every time

*"They might ask you to sing. **Learn to sing**!"* Learn it as you learn to play your instrument. Many of the truths we've covered apply to your voice as much as any other instrument. And there is one more reason to learn to sing—to get the full experience! Uwe once told me, *"Don, my profession is really singing ... you won't make a living from playing an instrument alone if you don't sing, unless you're Chet Atkins."*

He's advocating the combination of playing and singing, and not just one over the other.

"The two go hand in hand. Play and sing if you want the full experience!"

The instrument is only half the story. **Learn to sing,** and you've got it all!

———

Instructions to a Five-Year-Old

"Every word you sing is like a conversation. Don't swallow the words; make sure you are understood. Be precise as if you're giving instructions to a five-year-old."

— *Uwe*

A song is a conversation. It's made up of a series of statements, questions or requests presented simply. Succinctly. Directly. Clearly. And—it's a conversation with a *kindergartener* apparently! Giving **instructions to a five-year-old.** Sometimes we get caught up in trying too hard and forget the basics. We try for a particular sound or attitude with our voice, and end up coming across as uncertain or unclear. Just get your teeth apart and sing a simple truth to a youngster!

When You Sing—Mean It!

"We've been lied to so many times we don't trust anyone anymore, so when you sing—mean it. We can tell a lie immediately. You cannot concentrate on lying and singing at the same time ... say something with your music—and mean it!"

— *Uwe*

When you sing—mean it. We can immediately tell a lie. Wow, I'd never thought of that. If I'm lying, they will know. Uwe's premise reflects my own worldview that we're being lied to all day every day in this so-called "civilized" world of television and the Internet. No? To me it appears there is no "news" without spin today. No simple reporting of events that don't include at least a non-verbal slant one way or the other. We take it for granted today. We're numb to it. Except that I'd never considered it within a musical context.

Remember our discussion of a creative sequence in setting the foundation for a song? Rhythm, melody, harmony. Maybe we need to add a fourth. Rhythm, melody, harmony, and *truth*. With intention we look to evoke an image, an emotion or action. When you sing, they can tell a lie. **When you sing— mean it!**

———

Whew, what a ride! I am *exhausted! Play. Practice. Create. Perform. Sing.* Ninety-four simple truths in music and life: from **Discover What You See** to **Put the Play in Playing Music**, to **What You Put into Your Life**, to **First Comes a Picture** to **Step Outside of Yourself** and all the way to **When you sing—mean it**. To close, I'd like to give you one last gift. It is a favorite quote of mine from a public speaker named Charlie "Tremendous" Jones:

"The only difference between who we are today and who we are five years from today, are the people we meet and the books we read."

For you I hope this book has been an experience deeply enjoyed, a gift you could never repay. "Simple Truths in Music and Life." In the telling of this journey, I too have been given the gift. I am forever transformed by the experience.

Thank you Uwe.

Journal Pages

Use the following pages to make your own notes.

66383731R00192

Made in the USA
Charleston, SC
20 January 2017